Leave no Marriage Behind!!!

Navigating the Trials & Tribulations for Lifelong Relationship Success

Leave no Marriage Behind
By Daniel & Michelle Faust

Designed by:
Victoria Ballweg
Dayton, Ohio

ISBN : 978-1-642047-62-2 (p)

Learn & Live

Scottsdale, AZ
623-321-4180
Info@learn-n-live.us

We mainly want to thank God for the strength and resources in this season to publish and the heart to press on despite multiple trials. Also, we thank Natasa Denman for teaching us how to publish via her "Ultimate 48hr Author" program. We had multiple contributors like Emily Palmer for the initial edit, Richard Burian for the transcription and partial editing, Christa Ferdako finishing the editing process, Victoria Ballweg for formatting the book for upload to IngramSpark, and the "USA 48hr author team" for the emotional support. Lastly, we thank the 27 people that took a risk on us to buy the book when this was only a concept. You all will be forever remembered because without you we wouldn't exist as authors.

THANKS FOR YOUR TIME AND BLESSINGS

Daniel & Michelle Faust

Introduction

When you google "Marriage" or "Marriage advice", the results are endless and especially these days it can come from many perspectives. For ourselves we wanted to give you timeless advice contextualized to today modern world. When you crack open this book we layout the book quite different from most marriage books. For your awareness, we will walk you through the layout so you understand how to read and apply this well.

First, right after the title and quote we immediate dive into five benefits why to apply our message from the chapters. We want to infuse the positive reasons in the beginning to build your hope for change. Then we address the negative consequences of not changing. At Learn & Live we rather walk you through wisdom than you hitting folly. This is for you to thrive and not just survive. After that, we give a unique stat or fact about the topic for your quiver (brain) to absorb. This primes the pump for the definition of the topic we are discussing so we all can be one the same page. Next, we over 3-4 tips to apply to your marriage in this area of life which is timely to today's world and principal based so it last the legacy of your marriage.

As with any tips or suggestions there are skeptics and we address that in the next section of the chapter and point out why this obstacles or barriers can be avoided. Lastly, we give you 3-4 action steps to take in this area of the your marriage so you can see lasting change. In these steps we recommend additional resources as applicable to the topic. We are not the subject matter experts in all areas but we give you the best resources we known at your disposal.

Our heart with this book to show you how love your spouse as the gospel calls us to do in the practical way. It can be drastically different if you know Jesus or his people but not both. If you have Jesus and not love his people, you relationship with your spouse will be difficult and you stay married out the principle and not heart. If you love people and not Jesus, you will affectionately love your spouse but not serve her well for a lifetime of marriage. Once trials come, it will the strength of the heart and will that determines the length of your marriage. Marriage is a covenant and not a contract. We hope to infuse a legacy view in your marriage for you to thrive in the trials and tribulations of life to carry into the generations to come.

Let's dive in into the refreshing pools of legacy to make your marriage thrive!

Table of Contents

CHAPTER 01

Till Death Do Us Part

Cornerstones are a key to long lasting buildings, which parallel the marriage to our spouse.

-Daniel Faust

In this book Leave No Marriage Behind, we will talk about the foundations of marriage. We want your marriage to last "till death do us part". The main benefit of staying married, and the foundations of marriage, is emotional intimacy. This is the key to connecting with your partner. Intimacy is an interesting word, because it sounds like "into me see", and we need to be emotionally connected with our partner. That's one of the benefits of marriage.

Marriage is a friendship that is long lasting, a friendship that keeps on going from start to finish. No matter if your marriage lasts 1 year or 80 years, each day is a day that friendship should increase.

Another benefit in marriage is that parenting is easier. It must be so difficult to be a single parent. The closest I (Daniel) have ever been to being a single parent was for about six weeks when my wife was working. It felt very daunting and I'm very thankful that we share parenting. Parenting is definitely easier, and a benefit in keeping a marriage.

Another benefit is sexual fulfillment and consistency. When you start dating you might get sexual fulfillment for a while, but it's not going to be long lasting. Marriage is a place where that sexual consistency can be ongoing.

And another one of the benefits is that you have a 180-degree picture to see 360 degrees around you. Each spouse sees different perspectives from left to right, up and down. So when there are two of you, you're able to see a 360-degree picture. When I was in a rush to fulfill my calling, my wife said to me, "Hey! Check out the facts!" It's definitely important to have a 360-degree picture.

A shocking fact that I found when researching this book is that the divorce rate for Christians is only 15-35%. What we can see from Shaunti Feldhahn's book, The Good News about Marriage, is that the divorce rate is not 50% as most people think. This number comes from the George Barna group, which cites a 1981 statistic spread across multiple demographics. That's the reason why everyone thought that number was true. However, if you live in a Christian home and go to church regularly, your marriage will typically only have a divorce chance of 15-35%. The goal of this book is to make it 0% – at least in your marriage.

Let's say you just don't care about the benefits I went over and listed. What's the contrast? What's the pain that would help you see otherwise? Obviously, if you don't keep building up a marriage, and you just keep on dating, then there will not be any commitment in your relationship. If you don't have that covenantal agreement to stay together, it's just based on emotions and justified with intelligence, which sets a lie. Cohabitation usually results in a 60% divorce rate upon marriage. It has been proven across the board to do that. Ultimately though, if you just want to live together, that is your choice.

When you cohabitate and then you decide to get married, you're more likely to get a divorce in that particular realm. But this book is not going to be about cohabitation. If you want to look into that then read The Meaning of Marriage by Timothy Keller, where he talks about that specifically.

Before we dive into the "how to" of marriage, how to keep it together, we need to have a definition of marriage. What is marriage? Our definition for this particular book is the following: "Marriage is one man & one woman coming together under the sight of God in a conventual relationship. Marriage represents our restored picture of God."

We come together to be in the sight of God, and then it shows a testimony, and a witness of the restored picture of God. Every time that a divorce happens, we tarnish that image of God in the eyes of the world.

You can see it for yourself if you've been through a divorce, or if you've been the victim of a divorce as a child. I know for myself (Daniel) that marriage was tarnished for me for a long time until I became a Christian. I actually had to learn the foundations of marriage. I won't go too in depth with the foundations of marriage, because this book is more focused on the practical principles. At this point you might want to briefly look at Genesis 3, 1 Timothy and also Ephesians; verses, which talk about the foundations of marriage. This will give you a good overall picture.

Let's talk about the "how to" of marriage, because this is going to be the in depth piece of this particular topic, and how to keep your marriage until death do you part. These are the first of 12 lessons we go through in each of the chapters.

Here is one strategy that you can use to understand the history and the origins of marriage, both biblically and practically. In a sense you need to go back to Genesis 3 where God brings Adam and Eve together to become one and to not be lonely, so he can have a partner and so she can have a partner. Practically, as we talked about earlier, God provided both of them with the 5 benefits and pleasures of marriage: emotional intimacy, friendship, joint parenting, sexual fulfillment and consistency as well as providing that 180-degree view that comes together to make a 360-degree picture. There's even more to it than that: being able to deal with hurts and healing.

That's God's history of marriage. It came from Genesis and was poured out over the generations. I definitely challenge you to get into His Living Word. Go into Genesis, Ephesians, and 1 Timothy to see more in depth on the origins of marriage biblically and practically speaking.

Here's a hypothetical story about a typical couple today. They hear in church over and over the false statistic that the divorce rate is over 50%. They live with the false belief that "our marriage is not going to last forever and turn into a legacy". From there they may get married, because of the emotional commitment, or some deeper psychological issues. They come together and they don't understand the foundations of marriage. They don't get counseling and then they walk out of marriage and get a divorce. Divorces take place on average at the 4-year mark. Essentially, did they train for divorce or did they train for something else?

On average, athletes train 4 years to go to the Olympics, but Christians don't train at all for marriage. We should not be training for divorce. When you see that the divorce rate is only 15-35% amongst Christians, it gives you a fighting chance and you can tell yourself, "We're a Christian couple, we can live through this." As we take you through each chapter you will learn how to live your marriage in a manner that leads to success and a fulfilled legacy.

No Commitment, based on just emotions, co-habitation usually results in 60% divorce rate.

The world we are living in seems very different to traditional marriage. In a secular state there are many different types of marriages. There is cohabitation, LGBT marriages and many other alternate lifestyles that seem at odds with the biblical description of marriage. Ultimately it is up to God, but this book focuses on marriage between one man and one woman, simply because I am called to live out his truth and to not shy away from it. We love everyone and don't want to leave you astray. Even if the state no longer holds traditional Christian marriage as the bedrock of society, Christians can still live long and healthy lives in a traditional Christian marriage.

Many Christians might be thinking to themselves that they have some objections to marriage, or have some specific problems with this subject. An objection that you might have, "What if I'm not sure if marriage is for me?" The first response to this is to go over the benefits that we talked about earlier: emotional intimacy, friendship, joint parenting, sexual fulfillment and the dream paradigm of being a team. Additional benefits are procreation as well as not being lonely.

Another objection you might have could be, "What if I no longer remember the reason why I got married?" Maybe you're frustrated with your partner? Maybe you're dealing with your marriage emotionally? Emotions are hard; emotions can wreck what we think. We have 70,000 thoughts a day and our emotions are a typical barometer of every single thought. When I get into arguments with my wife, I tend to be frustrated. I have thought at times, "Oh maybe I can get out of this situation, maybe I could go get a divorce, and then things would be easier." But if you take the time to deal with the frustrations of the different problems that happen in marriage, it will become better as time and work are poured into the marriage. It has been statistically proven that you are highly likely to improve in satisfaction as your marriage progresses if you make the effort to deal with frustrations and problems as they come up. This is usually seen within 5 years or less in your worst trials

As you go and live out this legacy of going past all the frustrations and remember the reason why you first got married. It's very important to do that. You need to reflect on that on a daily basis. Our personal recommendation is to write notes down reflecting the reasons why you wanted to get married. That might help you with the objections on how to deal with those frustrations, and to remember in those frustrations. They're in the moment, and most of the time as we talk about in future chapters, they're based on communication, on how to deal with conflict resolution, understanding your partner sexually how to live a legacy for your marriage, etc

We'll be going through these concepts and more in future chapters.

Another objection you might be thinking is that you think marriage is a piece of paper, "Why do I need it?"

Let's go from the secular view, first off. There's a ton of financial benefits in being married. That's not the primary motivation, but just think of it logically. The average couple that makes under $100,000 is going to benefit in taxes and combining their income into reduced down resources is more fruitful. The statistics show that 98% of people are going to get married. God has that perfect design, that we still have an urge to get married.

The legal piece of paper gives us contractual and conventual safety. A contract is an "if-then" statement. If you do this then I do this. If you don't do this then I'm going to do this. This is why it's so easy to get divorced when you just have a contract. If you stop feeling emotionally connected then you can just leave.

A covenant, however, binds us in two ways. It binds us emotionally, and it binds us in a command. Which means, this is a statement that's iron clad. So when my emotions are not there in the marriage, I have the command to follow. When the command is the only thing that sustains me, then the command over time will change my emotions.

This is very important to understand because as humans we need both to thrive in our marriages. If we don't have both, only have one, or none are marriage is a time bomb into divorce.

You can look at more in depth definitions as you read into Genesis and Exodus in covenantal agreements. I recommend you study those two books of the Bible.

I want to challenge you with three actions that you, the reader, should take as a result in reading this chapter.

1) Go and take a moment in your day to think about why you got married. A moment is only 6 seconds, so I definitely want to challenge you for more than 6 seconds. I want you to take that moment in your day and every day as you dwell in your heart to ponder on why you got married. It's going to keep you focused on the legacy of your marriage, and why God has called you to get married in the first place. Even if you weren't a Christian when you got married, God had a specific reason why you married that particular spouse at that particular time.

2) I want you to discuss your reasons with your spouse and vice versa, with their permission. We tend to think that just because we're married we have this automatic permission to just get into deep conversations whenever we feel like it. But we need to respect their boundaries via their permission. If we go and assume that we have permission, usually it turns into an argument. Then it turns into more frustration and then you're going to go back into objections like: What if I no longer remember the reason why I got married? I'm just frustrated with my husband or wife. When we discuss our why we are with our spouse and vice versa, and get permission we have a new fuel for the fire of marriage.

3) This is the huge one and it's going to take time. I recommend you write this down. I recommend you write all these three things

down, circle them in your book, whatever you need to do. READY??? I want you to start with the end in mind. What do I mean by that? We tend to go and get married with the "happily ever after" in mind. You go on dates, you have an emotional high, you're attracted to each other, you might even desire to be with them more than dating and then one day you say, "Hey we like each other, we get along with each other, do you want to get married?" Then you get married and then you realize that the first day was the most important. You planned that out and spent tens of thousands of dollars on a wedding. The average wedding now is between $25-$30,000, but we don't plan for the legacy on the last day, when your partner will pass away. You don't see or think about what the last day looks like. It's better to think about this the other way around.

So what I want you to do with this question is to start with the end in mind. Look 5, 10, 15, 20, 30, 40, 50, 80 years down the road. What is your legacy? What are you going to bring to the table? What has God called you to do? These things you're going to be doing in your marriage; that you should be thinking about years down the road.

For myself I'm looking for a condo, or buying out a house in this season. I'll be thinking about whether this house will sustain our family. Will I be able to go and function in this house 50 years down the road? Even in housing, we tend to not look at legacy. Most people buy the house for the kids. Then 20 years go by and our 50s and 60s hit us, we become frail and sometimes sick and then we are selling the house. For me I'm looking at the legacy of our marriage. I think about things like whether I'll be able to take care of my wife when I'm 85. I think about whether I'll be able to take care of my adult children in their relationships. Will I be able to have my grandkids over? Even my great, great grandkids? Will I be able to function?

What is your legacy? Have you thought about that?

I'm going to end the chapter with that. Take these three actions. I'm going to ask you to go and think about these actions, pray about them, and write these actions down. Take some time with your spouse, and I hope to see you again in the next chapter to go over and make your marriage a legacy from start to finish.

CHAPTER 2

People Puzzles

If you understand me and I understand you, doesn't this mean we will have a better relationship?

-DR ROBERT ROHM, (PARAPHRASED)

As we jump into relationships and marriage, every relationship is a people puzzle that we just don't understand. We go from opposites attract to opposites attack. What's the benefit of understanding me and understanding you in a relationship? One of the benefits is eliminating pitfalls. Instead of diving in and being like, 'woops, I fell into that...' if I understand you and you understand me we're going to eliminate those pitfalls as much as possible.

Another benefit is knowing your strengths, because everybody has different strengths and different giftedness. When you understand that you can work better and say, 'hey, I work in this way, you work in this way, let's come together and you work on this portion and I work on that portion.'

Another benefit is overcoming your weaknesses. Rather than having your spouse point out your weaknesses, you can discuss each other weaknesses as a observable behavior. This allows less emotional blaming and empowers you work with each in your weaknesses. Even potentially overcoming it.

The biggest reason to understand yourself and understand others, especially in marriage, is to minimize the conflicts. They're going to happen, but if we can minimize them we can be better and have less stress.

Lastly is learning to fight well, because conflicts will come and if we're equipped to understand ourselves and others, we can fight well and then speak well and then have a thriving relationship.

One of the very interesting facts I teach as a behavioral consultant and also a marriage consultant is that 90% of your conflicts start due to people's different priorities and we'll get into that in a little bit. Think about that, 90% of your conflicts are due to people's different priorities.

Let's say you don't care about this, let's say this is something where you're like; I don't need help in communication, I don't need help in understanding myself, I already understand myself. Well, you will tend to fight for yourself instead of the relationship if you want to go with this model and over time you will go from having a face to face relationship, and that's how we date, we sit face to face in restaurants, we go places to talk and eventually as we go over and get married we go shoulder to shoulder. Hey, let's go work together on certain projects or what not and that works well for a season. Especially with men. Men relate better this way, typically. But eventually shoulder-to-shoulder then returns to back to back. And for back to back, sometimes it happens in parenting, in the job market, in different things, but most importantly, if it keeps going back to back, you're going to keep walking away from back to back, which leads to emotional and/or physical divorce.

You'll get so far from back to back, one day you'll turn around and what will happen is you'll realize, I don't know who the hell this person is, so why am I going to stay? It's been hurting so bad, we've just been barely functional, we took care of the kids for 10-15-20 years, they're self sustaining, they're manageable, so why stay together?

Again, we do need a mixture of all of the face-to-face, shoulder-to-shoulder and back-to-back. There's going to be moments where we're need to work together via back to back but if this becomes the norm it will destroy the marriage just by not understanding your spouse. The biggest divorce reason out of the top 10 is usually communication. Why not work through that communication problem and gap?

E/I sets the lie while I/E sets your free

-Dr. Robert Rohm

We have to have a clear definition to work through communication. What is communication? Communication is a means of connecting between two or more people. Yes, guys, we have to connect. Women usually connect a lot better than this, that's why I emphasize that. Our marriage should be and is called to display and live out the deepest connection. That's the example we're supposed to go and live out day to day.

I know in the deepest of your being that you don't want to

just live a surviving marriage, because you wouldn't have purchased this book and you wouldn't have picked it up in reading this specific chapter and maybe you even skipped to this chapter, just to get some advice and some thoughts behind how to communicate better.

Let's jump in and talk about how to do that.

First things first, you've got to have a baseline for communication. We're going to actually use the DISC model of human behavior as our bones for that and also we are certified from Personality Insight, so we're going to be using their material to glean off and then adding our own perspective.

Let's go dive in.

First things first, you have to understand that we have a motor and people have different types of motors. Actually there are two. Are you more outgoing or are you more reserved? Are you the person that likes to hang out with a bunch of people? Likes to be in front of the limelight? Likes to just go do a bunch of things? Or are you the person that is at home watching movies, watching Netflix and just chilling in the house? We wax and wane between outgoing and reserved, but that's the first question you need to answer for yourself, are you outgoing or more reserved?

The next question you have to answer is the priority question. Are you more task oriented or people oriented? Let me go into a story. In the military when you live on base, one of the many requirements is to mow your lawn and to keep it in a certain regulation. If you're more task oriented, you'll be like a field marshal going out and saying, yeah, I'm going to get this done and do it this way and measure this out and I'm going to have all these little things and I'm going to meet the requirements. So, somebody comes over and starts talking to you when you are mowing the lawn and you are like, "Oh gosh (choose your phrase lol), I just want to get the task done". So you can either do one of two things, you can push the person to help you get the task done or try to push the person away to get the task done. That's a version of a task-oriented person.

Let's say, same story, different personality style. Now you're more people oriented. You've still got to get the lawn done, because you're in the military, but you're more people oriented. You should be getting up at 5:30 doing the lawn when it's nice and cool, but you get up at 8:30, get ready by 10:30 and then you're like "I've just got to mow this lawn, this sucks". So someone comes over and starts talking to you and you're like, "Look a friend, I'm so excited" and you don't even know this person is from Sunday. If you're more outgoing and people oriented, you're going to talk to them for about 3 hours, take them inside, go drive a car, go do something and you never get the lawn done. If you're more reserved and people oriented, you let them lead the conversation, you might or might not get a task done because that person has taken/ monopolized your time. Later on,your spouse rips you about not finishing the lawn and you use your people oriented skills to get out of the argument.

Which ones are you? Are you more outgoing or reserved? Task or people oriented?

You don't have to commit to this, it's not a specific covenantal thing, we just want to give some extremes so you can understand the basics of communication. Once you answer those two questions, now you can understand the DISC model behavior.

Let's get into the first style, the first style is outgoing and task oriented. I'm going to listen the characteristics of this style and want to see if you resonate with this style. Do you feel dominant? Are you direct? Do you tend to be demanding? Do you like to be decisive? Are you very determined and are you a doer? And do other people tell you that you are a tad defiant? The words again are dominant, direct, demanding, decisive, determined, doer and defiant.

If you resonate with this style you wake up in the morning and you just want to go get things done. You might not get it done right, but you're going to go get it done. You'll get more done 9-5 than most people. Again, accuracy, that's a different story.

You are very demanding of people's time and you're very demanding of getting things done. You're very decisive when you make decisions. You don't take too long on anything. You're very determined on whatever direction you're going, you're much of a doer, just want to do do do, get it done and you can be a tad defiant while getting it done. You'd rather ask for forgiveness than go over and ask for permission.

If you resonate with this style, you're the dominant style.

Now let's go into the next style. Outgoing and people oriented. Here are some words and questions for you.

Do people tell you that you're inspiring? Are you very much an influencer? Are you very impressionable or very impressionable to others? When you hang out with people are you very interactive, do you move your hands? Are you very animated? Are you very impressive? Are people impressed at what you do and what you say? Like for myself I do the one hand clap. (You have to see this in person because I'm not going to go clap on the microphone). Also are you interested in people? Lastly, and this is caution word, just like defiant was, are you a tad illogical? Do you go over and shoot first and then figure it out? Do you find out later you were wrong afterwards?

If you resonate with being inspiring, influencing, impressionable, interactive, impressive, interested in people, and a tad illogical as your primary style, then you are an inspiring person and this is how you communicate.

Let's go into the next style. If you've answered the questions and think you're more reserved and people oriented, then you are a very S type, supportive type. Here are the questions I'm going to ask.

Are you very supportive in what you do and with the people that you're with? Do you have a stable life and stable platform that you like to thrive in? Are you very steady? Do you get called a steady Eddy? Are you a very sweet person? Do you seem to do the status quo? Are you very shy? One of the caution words I want to give you, just like every other style has, do you tend to be a tad of a sucker? The words again are supportive, stable, steady, sweet, status quo, shy, and can be a tad of a sucker.

If you resonate with this style, you tend to be very sweet and everybody loves you. "Status quo" is that you like to do the same thing every day. I had one guy in my life that ate a roast beef sandwich at 11 o'clock at work every single day. I had to go rush for a briefing, he's like, 'I need to warm up my sandwich.' I'm like, 'dude let's go.' You can be very shy, these people are not the people that come up and say, "Hey, how are you doing, my name's so and so". They're not going to talk that way; they'll talk to you as they warm up to you. What we mean by the word "Sucker" is they tend to not say no. They'll say yes to most things just to appease and keep that peace. Do you resonate in that style? If you do, you're the S type.

And the last type, if you've answered the questions and you feel that you're primarily more reserved and more task oriented, this is the cautious style. Let's see if these questions resonate with you. Do you feel or tend to be more conscious? Do you calculate things before making decisions? Are you very competent in the areas that you're in and only focused in those areas? Are you very conscientious in your decisions? When you think are you very contemplative and are you very careful with the people you connect with, decisions that you make and the thoughts that you have? Lastly our caution word, do you see yourself or do other people see you as a tad cold?

Lack of communication leads to a lack of trust that leaves room for doubt

-Amen Amare'

The words again are cautious, calculating, competent, conscientious, contemplative, careful and can be a tad cold.

These people are the think tanks, these are the people that are usually engineers or scientists. They're very careful emotionally, mentally and even spiritually. These people are cautious before buying or committing to something or someone. These people won't work or try something unless they have a deep understanding. They will mull over their thoughts in their head and typically write most things down to wrestle with later. Lastly, they can be a tad cold because their emotions are not displayed on their face/body languages. It is hard to read if they are mad, sad, angry, or wanting a hot dog.

Do you resonate in any of these styles? We are a blend of everything and you might need to think about these things. I'm also going to give you some actions for you to take and challenge you to learn more about this, because this is key. As we talked about earlier, 90% of the conflicts start due to people's different priorities.

Your priorities, which we didn't clarify too much about, are tasks versus people. The other 10% is actually if you're more outgoing or more reserved. Whenever you do have problems, 90% goes towards priorities, tasks and people, 10% goes to outgoing and reserved. Think about those things.

Once you have a basic understanding of the DISC model of human behavior, you might have some objections. You'll also might have some objections because review of the DISC model of behavior is very quick. We're going to give you some resources to dive more in.

One objection to this is, "I am wired a certain way and I can't change". That's actually false. Yes, you are a certain personality style but the goal is not to change is who you are, but how you respond? When you're in control of the Holy Spirit you will display the good qualities of your personality and refute the out of control characteristics. If you're familiar with the Bible think of Saul and Paul. Saul never changed his personality style, he changed his character and who had control of him. The Trinity had his heart and God used his personality to love many to Christ.

The next objection that you have is that this is just too hard and doesn't feel natural. Well, maybe you're right, but just as your kids might say the same things for chores, it is still necessary to keep up a house. If we don't allow filth in our house, why would you allow that for your soul? Anything out of control we allow is like filthy rags to our soul and we just spew that on others.

I know for myself I really struggled with sarcasm when I first got married, up until about year 7 and that was out of control. The Holy Spirit gave me a visual of sarcasm which I will share. Sarcasm translates to tearing of flesh. My wife said that my sarcasm was like tiny little razor cuts all over her body. God gave me a visual of her standing in position getting cut from invisible forces and bleeding everywhere and crying why. For me, that totally changed me and I learned this model to save my marriage, because I can understand all the vertical principles (Godly principles from the Bible) and we'll talk about some of those in the book. But if I don't understand the horizontal principles (face to face communication with people) in a relationship, which God wants us to understand, you will destroy your marriage even if you understand about all the Biblical stuff in the world. We've got to have a balance of both! Understand God's general revelation(is the things that it brings in front of us, communication, the weather, things of that nature) and specific revelation(the Gospel).

Maybe another objection you have is that you don't have time to learn this, you've got bigger fish to fry. How often do you budget in having conflicts in your marriage? For myself, I have lost countless hours of time and emotional strength because I didn't put the priority of loving my spouse. We're going to talk about that more in Chapter 11 about getting your doctorate degree in your spouse, but this is the start. You can just take 10-15 minutes, it can add much abundance in your life and your marriage. It's your call. It's your marriage. You got this book for a reason, so maybe take a little sacrifice, a little challenge each day to thrive. It will be worth it!

Here's 3 actions I want to recommend you guys as readers as a result of the chapter.

1) If you see right below, we're going to have some links for you and one of the first challenges I want to give you is to take our four lessons of better relationships. This will go more in depth than what I just went through in the book. Click on the link, add an email address and we will give you four free lessons on a better relationship to understand more about the DISC model of behavior and your primary style. We give you broad strokes here, I want you to get more in depth outside of here.

www.personality-insights.com/resources/?ref=52

2) My next challenge to you is the challenge to learn more about yourself by completing a personality assessment. The link is below and you're going to save 10% because we're affiliated to Personality Insights. This profile and time in the word has saved my marriages and relationships and I want the same for you. We have several types for all budgets. If you have questions on the store, our contact info is in the back of the book and on the back cover.

www.personality-insights.com/shop/?ref=52

3) Last but not least, my last challenge to you if you really want to learn about your spouse, schedule a consultation with us. We'll take your profile, her profile, put that in a relationship feedback report. After that, we will go over that with you in consultation contextualized to you in person, live video, or over the phone. Specifically for people reading this book, you can reference that you read the Leave No Marriage Behind book, we will reduce our consultations. Our readers save 25-50% per hour. Again, our contact info is in the back of the book/back

cover.

Hope to see you guys in Chapter 3. Thanks for your time.

CHAPTER 3

Unlocking Differences

Natural disasters and conflicts have two things in common, they can be predictable or unpredictable based on knowledge and the devastation you experience will be based on what you do with this knowledge, which is wisdom.

-Daniel Faust

As we go over unlocking differences, we have to understand conflict. Conflict is what most humans avoid, especially 25-35% of the population as we talked about earlier in Chapter 2, but did you know that there are actually benefits to conflict? Some of the benefits that you have with conflict are that you develop a new respect. You get to see a viewpoint that someone didn't show before, so you can respect them for where they stand. Another benefit is expressing new ideas and issues, because we tend not to do this as we're having normal conversation; we don't express them, but when we have conflict those new ideas and issues tend to bubble to the surface.

Another benefit in conflict is the opportunity to show empathy. The difference between sympathy and empathy is, If someone got hit by a car and I was to I can be sympathetic. Sympathy is generated emptions relating to the situation because both parties have gone through similar situations. The key word is similar. Take the same situation but I haven't been hit by car, I can generate feelings of what it is like to go through the situation. That's empathy and we can do the same in conflict and be empathetic to the person that has whatever said issue. Also, a another unique benefit to conflict is actually to bring harmony, because once we come together and bring the issue to the surface, we can eventually come to harmony together. One of the biggest things that conflict can do is to bring growth and intimacy. We can handle more, love better, and be deeper connected once we choose to roll into the conflict and finish it well.

I know for myself that any time I have arguments with my wife (it's a when, not an if) that we have a chance to grow together and grow more intimate. We get more deeply connected, so we can work those things out. We talk more about conflict resolution in Chapter 04, but these are at least some of the benefits of conflict.

One of the shocking truths that I've seen is that if we avoided conflict, we wouldn't have had our nation, most of our ideas, inventions and even this book. This book for me has been an internal conflict, seeing on why divorces have been around me and having the burden to do something about it. This is the first time that I(Daniel) can give something tangible to you all to learn from. Our goal is for you all to know, like, and trust us, so that we can help you shoulder that burden of helping your marriage, so we can leave no marriage behind.

What's the contrast? When we look at marriage, we want no conflict. When you eliminate that you can get rid of the most precious elements of conflict. Do you know what that is? It's called growth, people! It's called growth. We're in denial all the time, but that's what conflict does. It challenges us to grow, even as a kid walks and stumbles, if I continue to pick them up, they'll never learn. They'll need to be in conflict until the point when they are burdened enough to walk.

We want to do the same for you in your marriage, to walk and then run, to go from surviving to thriving. The best definition that we've found so far of conflict that I've heard is the following.

Conflict is an inevitable, unavoidable part of our every day, professional and personal lives.

We're going to add a little bit to this definition and the closer the proximity of the person that you live with, the stronger on the inevitable and the unavoidable part becomes. This is in essence the shocker moment. You and your spouse need to be aware of the "when and not the if".

Confrontation should always leave a person's dignity intact

-A.J Anglin

Let's go jump into the how's and how conflict happens and maybe some pitfalls of it.

The honeymoon phase:
If you've been married more than 6 seconds, the honeymoon phase is like, 'hey everything's fine, intimacy's great, we're all lovey dovey and everything'. For us, that didn't last that long. In a matter of the first couple of months, I went through my first deployment and then (Michelle) was really vulnerable and then reality hit fast. We tend to put on a mask for a bit in this season, Christians or not and then when we get safety and security in the marriage, we become who we really are.

I started seeing so many different things in my spouse and

in that first deployment I was wrestling, in conflict, on a regular basis with my spouse and I was wrestling with divorce in the first 4 months. I got married, had lots of conflicts, got told I'm moving work centers, got told that I'm deploying to a foreign country and having a baby. I was just newly married and all these other things came up. Definitely conflict can come out even in the honeymoon phase. That first deployment for me was huge. This series of conflict started me (Daniel) on my calling, specifically this, and learning about how to communicate and love my spouse better.

Another thing that we need to understand about conflict is that anything can trigger it. Conflict is unavoidable. Here's a little funny story that did it for us. Have you ever done laundry before? You probably have. We did laundry on a regular basis, about year 5 we were down in Arkansas at the time; I've had a lot of moves, about 35, shock for a moment. But anyway, we had this move, we moved down to Arkansas and we were doing laundry. I(Daniel) go over and do the laundry: I fold the laundry, put it away, hang it up, it's in order. Michelle had these 'pile systems'. This was one of the most explosive arguments I ever had in my life. So many 'you are' statements, which are accusatory, I blame shifted everything, we got into such a horrible fight, it was 3 days of so stupid of a thing. It still is amazing that we went back and forth talk about how laundry should be done. I wanted to fold and she wanted to do 'pile systems'. They're not right, they're not wrong, they're just different. I did not realize that. I was getting into a

Reverence reduces hostility

-TOBA BETA

fight, willing to put my morality on the line, willing to die for this, for laundry. Absolutely anything can trigger a conflict, even laundry. We eventually went over to a system where we used piles, but I put them in drawers, so we came to a compromise. Then a couple of years later she started folding clothes again. Again conflict goes in ebbs and flows. Even though it might be a minor conflict sometimes, I'm not going to allow that to destroy me, but absolutely anything can trigger a conflict; so be prepared for that, be wise in that. Don't assume that certain areas are for safekeeping. We need to be ready to understand that anything can trigger it.

Another thing that you might need to ponder on is this concept that we were naive on (in dating, during premarital counseling, and even in the first little bit of marriage) is Christianity doesn't block conflict. You can come to Jesus, both are Christians and having a Biblical marriage and the conflicts will still come. A Biblical marriage is not going to shield you from the conflicts. It was year 7, we moved back to Washington State and were struggling with jobs and I think I've had about 15 jobs at the time. It was June of 2013 with 7 years of marriage, walking in the faith, active in church, and we almost walked into a divorce for the sheer stupidity of conflicts. We were going to take that moment, specifically me(Daniel) and be selfish,sinful and destroy a marriage. A marriage with 4 kids, 7 years, 4 deployments, dealt with mental health, spiritual health, physical health issues, almost a couple of deaths, losing parents (emotional toxic relationships) etc. We were going to take that, specifically me(Daniel) and toss that in a hamper. God has had through all this and just toss away from job problems. The trials will come and conflict will spike and at the same time he is faithful to be there. (We know!!!) What will you choose?

I recommend reading the Good Fight by Dr Les Parent and they really go in depth of how to deal with conflict. In the next chapter we talk about dealing with conflict, so this would be a culmination of Chapter 3 and Chapter 4, so we're just gleaning from all these different resources.

Maybe one of the objectives that you have is that "I'm the passive type and want to avoid conflicts, so why engage in it?" Yes. You might be the peacemaker of the particular relationship. You might just think that you can avoid these things and it's a great quality that peacemaker, but most times inside it will eat you alive. You will just shove, shove, and shove until you explode. It's better to vent the steam off like a teapot than become that unpredictable bomb.

Just an FYI, we use extreme example to get your attention like most of the postal shooters in the '80s and '90s were the sweet passive ones that wanted to avoid conflict. It will happen, so make sure you're venting off your pot.

Another objection that you might go through is that you saw conflict destroy your parents' marriage and it will not destroy mine, so we choose happiness instead. Happiness I agree is a great emotion, but conflict unresolved can easily be rooted in sin, bitterness, etc is not healthy and the happiness will become a façade if not dealt with. We're going to talk about this in the next chapter, of how to have good fights.

Last, I love to debate, argue, and have a good fight once in a while is great. So why change it.

As I talked about in the communications chapter, about People Puzzles earlier, you might be that high, dominant personality we talked about earlier. You're dominant, your decisive, you can be a doer; you can be a tad defiant, you like a challenge, and this style is about 10%.

Since you are only 10% of the population it is unlikely you married the debating type. So unless you're okay of being alone in marriage and just being the King of the mountain it might be high time to reorient your thinking.

As usual, we have three actions that you, as the reader should take as a result of reading this chapter and here's some resources for you to get more in depth on these topics.

1) I want you to ponder on the reality that conflict is real and to accept the realities of it in your lives. If you don't accept conflict is going to happen on a 'when' then it's going to become explosive and destroy you. That's what's actually going to happen; you'll avoid, avoid, avoid, shove, shove, shove, explode, explode, and explode. You need to understand the realities of life that you need to have conflict every once in a while. There are benefits that we talked about earlier. If you don't have conflicts you won't develop that new respect, express those new ideas and issues, have empathy for your partner, come to a harmony and then grow and then have better intimacy. You won't be able to do that.

2)My next challenge to you is to figure out what type of person you are in conflict? Are you the passive or active one? Go back to chapter 2 and ask yourself this question: "Which personality style am I?" If you are the more dominant in conflict, you tend to get physically and verbally hostile. Are you that type of person in conflict? If you're more inspiring in conflict, you tend to blame shift? If you are more supportive in conflict, you tend to stonewall, tend not to deal with it and potentially go to sleep in conflict to avoid it. If you are more conscientious in conflict, you tend to be critical. You point out all the facts in a critic backbiting way and potentially lose the person.

What type of person are you in conflict? Are you passive or are you active? If you don't know, then again go back and reread chapter 2, go buy a personality profile, buy some books we reference in our "Resources" page, schedule a consultation. This will open your eyes to your wiring. I guarantee you it opened up mine when I was deployed.

3) Take 5 of the conflicts that you have had whenever, recently, years ago and reflect back how you responded in that situation. Was it good? Was it bad? Be ready with them for the next chapter on Working it Out.

Conflict is a "when" not a "if" so take the time to soak up the benefits and after that dive into the next chapter to resolve it well.

Fight well

CHAPTER 4

Working It Out!!!

Whenever you're in conflict with someone there is one factor that can make the difference between damaging your relationship and deepening it. That factor is in attitude.

-WILLIAM JAMES

Working it out in conflict resolution has several benefits, because you're thinking, what's the point of working out conflict, I'm already in conflict, why do I want to go deeper into it? Some of the benefits are:

1) Deepening the relationship. As you work out these conflicts, you get to know the person, you get to know their heart and because you have it will deepen the connection which will deepen the relationship.

2) Another benefit is that it allows you to celebrate and appreciate the differences. If you're in conflict, you're just dividing, you're intolerant and on elimination – when you actually get through the conflict you can celebrate the victory of the resolution and now you can appreciate the person's differences. As you appreciate the

differences you can celebrate the differences and then you are more uniquely bonded together.

3) Another benefit is also breaking the patterns. We want to break that cycle. There's a book called the DNA of Relationships by Dr Gary Smalley, he talks about cycles and patterns of arguments which unchecked can become a cycle of abuse. When we do conflict resolution, we're breaking those patterns, we're breaking those strongholds and God wants us to go over and break those patterns because those patterns are not of Him.

4) Another thing that is a benefit is that it brings us unified and brings oneness together. We have unity together and we have oneness together as we grow together but if we are in conflict we are divided. When you resolve something, you're bringing two broken people back together as one in Christ as the intermediary of that. When you go and resolve together, you bring each other back together through him.

5) Conflict resolution brings in the element of humility. Humility is to put yourself in a right place where God has you. It doesn't make you haughty and prideful, it doesn't make you live in despair. Either direction is not of God and brings division amongst his people. Especially in marriage we need humility and this needs to be the safest and first place to display this characteristic. If we can't display it here, how much harder will be it be with our children, other family members, friends, and enemies. Humility, which is a benefit, is also the key to keeping your relationship.

Maya Angelou comment on conflict was so profound that I wanted share with you Her quote summarized is that people don't remember what you said, most of the time all they remember is how you made them feel. We remember the emotions of the argument more than the intellectual words of that conflict. What's the contrast if we don't resolve conflict? The average person feels separation in conflict, as well as isolation, anger and fear when conflict is not resolved. With all these emotions combined, it doesn't make Captain Planet, but Major Resentment. (Hahaha, tried to make you laugh).

Before we jump into conflict resolution, we need to have a universal definition just like we do in every chapter, so that we can all be on the same page regarding conflict resolution. Conflict resolution is the process of ending a conflict by cooperating, compromising, sacrificing, letting it go, giving it to God and problem solving to restore the relationship and hopefully growing into intimacy deeper than before you started.

How do we do that? I will my life as a example of how to resolve conflict. My wife stays home all days with our 4 children when they were toddlers. I would work all day via the military from 7am to 5pm or later. I would assume with her being home with 4 little hands that the chores would be finished or in a process of being finished. Most of the time, some things would be done but not all or there would be a explosion in certain sections of the home. Instead of just assisting in cleaning the chaos, I would rant while cleaning. The task would get done but my verbal throwup of sorts would erode in conflict or distance with my wife and my children. This was a major destroyer of emotional intimacy and brought major conflict. I had to learn how to communicate more softly and quietly with my wife to have her jump on board, make chores more like games with the kids, and most importantly to prime my mind and spirit on the ride home to prepare for all things and respond with his heart. As guys, we set the tone for the family, so we need to be sacrificial sometimes in our desires to show love to the family. Once I started to do this, it produced fruit. (These seasons will go in ebbs and flow so don't skip this practice when things go well)

Another how to resolve conflict is going over and giving it to God. For several years, I wasn't getting resolution in conflict and ranting was my solution. I call it the "ranty years" which was from year 1 to year 7. It took a major explosion argument to realize the damage I was doing for things that were not important and I could take over to do. This is when I had to realize if don't give it to God then I am taking his place which changes little to nothing. God answers prayer and never me so if you are running circles in conflict try to give in to God. It will be rough at first to pray but as time goes your heart will change and just maybe the resolution will come.

Sin, brokenness, and household work where my conflicts I threw into the marriage. I would just rant, rant, and rant. My wife for a long time had to give it to God, because my words were toxic. My words could have destroyed the relationship, if it wasn't for God holding it together. She gave it to God for years and it was at 7 years of marriage when we were on the brink of divorce, when we finally got to how much I suck and how much "I need Jesus".

Sometimes we are gifted to see flaws, problems, sin etc but it is not our job to point it out I did this in everyone's life and become that ranting dude. It doesn't edify. It's funny at first, especially if you're a third party person seeing this person rant and yell about the fridge being dirty or doing whatever else, but in the long run it just chips away at people. Some people are not going to challenge you right away & you're not going to see it. My wife had to deal with me, she needed to give that to God. If you are the person that's going and doing it, you need to take that introspective look asking yourself "Who am I in Christ?,, Who am I reflecting with others?, What things do I need to go and change?, and What do I need to give to God to be sanctified? This can be difficult amd scary thing, but the person on the other side is going to be way better and thankful for it. Again it's still something I'm growing in and we're all going to be doing that, but learn to give it to God both for the ranty person and the person taking the rant.

My last little 'how' is compromise. And I know you're thinking, 50-50 junk, that doesn't work. When you think of biblical compromise, it's giving of 100% and giving of 100%. It's just who's going to be the more mature person in that particular regard to compromise in that moment. We should be both giving of 100% to the marriage and that's why we need Jesus. So here's my other example for your good. We got married in 2006 and at first we had a lot in common but when you been married for a while you see that you have a lot of differences.

What counts in making a happy marriage is not so much how compatible you are, but how you deal with incompatibility

NURTURINGMARRIAGE.ORG

My wife laid cups down in the cabinets, so they wouldn't get dust in them. I was raised with cups up and we just constantly bickered about cups up vs cups down. We wasted hours on this issue. It was such a stupid argument that I don't remember the exact details of it. But the long story short is that we both came to compromise and for me specifically since it was my heart that was messed up, I went with her model. We both compromised and came to the conclusion what was best for our home and not what was displayed at our homes. Biblical compromise is what is best for the kingdom and his people. Let us compromise well.

We sometimes get into so many conflicts for such simple things that one of both of compromise. When we both give 100% to the marriage in Christ, we thrive instead of survive.

As you're thinking, you obviously have objections. We all do when we go over and read stuff. Let me go through some of them that I thought you might have.

Therefore what God has joined together, let not man separate

MATTHEW 19:6

Here's one, "What if I think I'm right?" Usually when people fight for what they think or know what is right, it is normally a value. A value is a highly sought ideal of your own formed over time. A moral is a standard of behavior you are usually willing to get hurt or die for. The question that you need to ask yourself is, "Are you willing to die for this? Are you willing to go to the brink of the cross and say, Jesus I am dying for the cups to be up instead of down?" Sometimes I would do that and it's sinful and wrong. Most times we fight for values not morals. You can give up the value. Let God change your values.

Another objection you might be thinking of is "I am done". Have you ever had that argument where you just go "I am done?" Stonewalling for a defined time is actually good for all parties, because it can escalate the conflict to sin; if you continually go into it, it never usually goes well. But in contrast if you take your stonewalling and upgrade it to building a wall, then it will just create deeper conflict and pain in the long run.

Being done is good for a season, but just don't be done for the long term. You're just digging more conflict and pain. And even if you go over and say, "Hey, I'm done and I want to get a divorce", that conflict and pain is still going to carry. In my previous generation of family, which is my mother and father, there are still certain parties that are in conflict and pain to this day and I think that there's walls in there.

Our last objection is: "If I admit that I am wrong, I will lose respect in the relationship". This I(Daniel) struggle with and usually men struggle with this. Typically men desire to be respected in marriage and women look for love. When this is not supplied, each spouse will stomp on each other's air hose (respect for men, love for the women). As you stick to being right, the respect air hose will not only be stopped but also take severe collateral damage. I can reflect on many arguments that at the end of my reign of rightness, I felt like a jackhole and respect was in the toilet. Sometimes you just need to be wrong, because sometimes being kind is better than being right.

Action plan time!! As we go broad strokes in this book, we want to equip you with plans to go deep after you are done with this chapter

1)Take a look at the book, Love and Respect, by Dr Eggeridge. It's a great little book that explains the love hose and respect hose. It gives you a more in depth look on how to live out love & respect in a practical way.

2)Have you ever had a relationship feedback report? This takes two personality assessments and merges them together to give each spouse a strength, struggles and strategies to grow their relationship. When you complete your personality assessments you can schedule this session with me for you and your spouse, so you'll have the link below and our contact information in the back to go over and to do that.

www.personality-insights.com/shop/?ref=52

3) Reflect back on the 5 most influential people in your life and see what good and bad strategies they've had for conflict resolution. Take the time to share these with your spouse again with permission to see how you can come together to squelch the fires of conflict when they arise.

Conflict resolution could be a great thing. It could help your relationship thrive instead of just survive, so as you're working it out, go dive into our next chapter to figure out more about your spouse and yourself to make your marriage thrive.

CHAPTER 5

Keeping It Fresh

Just as a litter box needs to be cleaned, your relationship needs a regular refresh or your whole relationship will just stink.

-Daniel Faust

It's a funny comment, but that's what happens. As we don't clean the litter box, over time it stinks and the happen it a relationship. So if we don't keep our relationship fresh, you and the litter box will have many things in common.

Some of the benefits of cleaning the litter box and also making your relationship fresh are less clumping (Not getting bored). Getting bored in a relationship can destroy it over time, and you try to go find fun things in other people than in your relationship. Sometimes you might be able to find it in the same sex, but typically we find it in the opposite sex. So if boredom sets it, we will go from face to face, shoulder-to-shoulder, and back-to-back in our relationships then we will part ways. As we're parting ways, we will see another person that's more fun, and happier (less clumpy) as start parting ways with that person.

The other benefit of cleaning the litter box/keeping the relationship fresh is it cleans the air When you keep it fresh, it keeps the relationship alive and you're happier. When you happier, you are more apt to want to come home, be with your spouse, and your children. If we're not happy with somebody we tend to avoid them. So let's get some cleaner air to stop this from happening.

The next benefit of cleaning the litter box/keeping it fresh is t that the relationship will become super absorbent.(resilient) . As the litter has super absorbency to take the impurities out, the same thing of keeping it fresh in a relationship helps us keep resilient in the relationship when trials comes. It keeps you going when things get bumped that you can't avoid.

Another benefit with this litter box analogy/keeping it fresh is that is eliminates dust (minimize problems). A dust free litterbox is inviting to the cat and so is a relationship that can little problems on the forefront. When you have a fresh relationship it is inviting and you want to solve the problems. If problems continue to be brought in without resolution and no variety/fun inbetween, you tend to avoid the relationship just like the cat avoids the box.

Last, there's no mess on the floor. This sustains oneness, so when the litter box gets really dirty, and just like your conflicts and your relationship as a whole. Things just get thrown on the floor, and even more junk is added. When you clean your litter box, just like you clean your relationship, it's going to sustain oneness; it's going to keep you together and keeps the relationship where it needs to be.

A shocking statistical fact is that we believe our wedding bands help prevent us from cheating on our spouse. According to The Truth

About Cheating, by M Gary Newman, nearly 70% of men who had an affair thought they would never do such a thing.

It happens because the complacency in our lives makes us go look for something new. We need to keep our marriage fresh on a regular basis.

What if we object to this and say "hey, my litter box is dirty, my relationship is dirty, and I just don't care." Just as you avoid changing the litter for your cat, if you breed complacency, don't be shocked to find crap in the weirdest places in your marriage. Cats go and do it too, and so can spouses, and so can your marriage.

Complacency
Just because things are going well now, doesn't mean they can't suddenly go horribly wrong

Complacency is a feeling of quiet pleasure or security, often which means being unaware of some potential danger, defect or the like, self satisfaction or smug satisfaction with an existing situation/condition etc. So basically in summary that complacency feels really good at first, but there's some potential dangers and defects that are in there. Then you go and put on pride that everything is okay and it's really not. There are things that are destroyed just like the litter box. If I don't smell it, it's okay; if I don't see it, it's okay. There are still looming things in that litter box, if you haven't cleaned it in two weeks.

Let's jump into how to keep it fresh in the relationship, and not breed complacency.

One example, which is usually the biggest area that we recommend, is to spice up your sex life. This is something I will talk more about in Chapter 9 "Under the Sheets" It is a real quick board strokes on sexual personality style. This doesn't go into biblically permissible acts though, so a good reference to find what is permissible in a Christian marriage sexually is Mark & Grace Driscoll, Real Marriage: The Truth about Sex, Friendship, & Life Together. This great book or audio book goes in great detail biblically about what is/not allowed morally, legally, and practically in your relationship.

Another thing to keep your relationship fresh is regular date nights. From Newsweek to other sources couples usually have sex 55-68 times a year. This is not even twice a week. Your date nights are probably less frequent than that. Typically most couples might have sex once a month, once every six months, on their anniversary, or on a major event. Especially if you have children or if there are other issues going on in the marriage such as financial issues or feelings of insecurity due to grief or other problems, or even just partners going through phases of life, there might be many reasons why couples make love infrequently.

When you have date nights it keeps the relationship fresh and typically increases intimacy.

So how do we integrate theses dates nights? I really think the first thing to do is, if you really want these regular date nights, number one you need to put it as a priority in your budget. You need to do that on a regular basis. You don't always have to do it on a Wednesday, with the same meal, going to the same place. If you and your spouse like that, and you're thriving, then that is great. If your spouse does not like that then you need to break up the variety.

I would recommend at least 50-100 bucks, probably once ever

two weeks. Try doing some free ones if you need to. This is a a must in some capacity to keep the marriage fresh. We understand that finances and schedule can be difficult (4 kids under 11) so we wanted to give you a recommendation So if the kids, the schedule, and just life are bounding and you can't get it, you can go over to Datebox.com. This site basically builds your date all out and plans it and they mail it to you once a month. The first month is typically free and then I think it's between $40-$60 a box, but you can go and split that, parts of it into four separate weeks and now they offer virtual datebox in a app for approximately $10 a month. It's very creative, gives you the instructions, gives you the tools. In one box there was popcorn, in another kit there was ingredients to learn how to roast coffee together. They give many different options for bonding activities. It's not a subscription; you can do it from month to month and cancel it any time.

I highly recommend it. Dr Les Parrot introduced my partner and I to it when we went to one of their fight night seminars. It's definitely worthwhile.

Another suggestion to keep it fresh in your relationship is to break the tyranny of urgency. What does that mean? The tyranny of the urgent is a concept that most Americans live out. We will work or do what is pressing in front of us and not work on the important things. This concept can help us evaluate in Christ what things we are you doing, is it important compared to urgent, and then decide which things to take on. Most of the time you're doing a lot of urgent things, and they're not important things. You can evaluate these things in hindsight and learn from them.

An example in our marriage is that when my wife calls me

towards the end of day and remembers an item we need for home like milk. It is urgent because the kids eat cereal in the morning. So I (Daniel) scramble to the military grocery store hunting for this one item which takes 30 minutes to 1 hr of time. I then come home with less time to focus on home tasks, my wife, kids, etc. When we jumps through hoops to get the urgent done, we push aside the important things to get done. Sometimes it delays the important things and sometimes it can take the important times with people. We need to protect the things, time, and people that are important to thrive.

An example that I've taken recently to break the cycle is the following: I told my wife that I need to plan each and every day so the urgent is avoided is possible. Let's say I leave the base at 4:30 PM and I get a text at the last second asking me to get something on the way home. Instead of going to save the day to get the item. I now evaluate the situation together to see if this is urgent or important. If urgent then I tend to put on the next day agenda. This puts it back into the important category instead of urgent, because we get 86,400 seconds in a day and we can't get those back.

The complacency of fools destroys them

PROVERBS 1.32-33

If you're a math wiz and you want to know minutes, it's 1440 minutes, 24 hours in a day, and we don't get that back.

We need to evaluate our lives together to find out what's important compared to urgent. That's what I recommend you go to read Tyranny of the Urgent. This book has helped me hugely in my relationship. I don't get caught up in all this stuff that everybody else does. I have four kids and people are like, you must be super busy? I choose the important things to do; I don't choose the urgent things to do so I am not busy. I am only busy with the important things

Again, I'm not perfect, but I try and do this as best as I can on a daily basis. It's really in my heart. If you know me, and get to know me you'll see that it is.

Just like every chapter, you're probably going to have objections. We all do; every single book we read. So let's just get right into them.

First objection is, "I don't like new things. I like just doing the same thing over and over again like roast beef sandwiches at 11 AM, every day. You might like the same schedule and routines. This might work well for you, but generally your spouse will be the opposite. You might think life is smooth sailing, but like the litter box, the mess can sneak up at any moment.

As you keep things fresh, you'll find it's easier to deal with life's circumstances, and you can build new memories at the same time. You might find out some new things you like that can guarantee your routines are win-win for all.

Another objection might be is "Keeping it fresh is so draining. That is why I got married, so I could just have those routines. Dating was hard". Marriage is a living and breathing organism, and like anything in life, things change. You don't need to change absolutely everything, but it's best to always take a check of your marriage.
I usually do it every 6-12 months on a big scale. I do a vector check(seeing if everything is working well) on a regular basis by myself. I probably go the extreme, so don't compare to me, but I would say every six months a year, do a vector check. Marriage maintenance is

way cheaper in the long run compared to a divorce, which is a massive drain on your life and any others attached. It will drain your children, your grandchildren, other family members and friends. It doesn't matter when you get the divorce; it's going to be a drain on your life.

Might as well keep it fresh instead.

Another objection that people often bring up is that you don't have any time to add another thing to your already busy life. You are so overloaded it takes you 9 months to go schedule with a friend. However, when you focus on the important things in life, keeping it fresh will be a lot easier. My life schedule has become so free understanding this concept, because I have the freedom to say no and as we talked about the personality styles earlier, the sweet, sensitive, stable person is going to be hard for you to say no. You're going to tend to be a sucker and tend to say yes. You need to learn how to say no, and then also say yes to your marriage. That's the biggest issue we all tend to have. Your marriage is the legacy, not the busy life for the schedule, no one's going to say, he was or she was the busiest person in the world, and that's what I'm rooting for. Your marriage needs to be a legacy first, and then the rest of life is an outpouring.

Here are three actions that you as a reader should take as a result of reading this chapter. I see these as huge. More than anything else, out of any of the chapters, these three are the top 3:

1) Take a bubble bath with your spouse. Do it at a hotel if you don't have a tub. Find out what weeds are in your relationship complacency routines. If there are any weeds, ask them to help you rip them out.

2) Plan a regular date night or order a date box and start

integrating regular time to a thriving marriage. This is going to make your marriage thrive in the long run. Spice it up too.

3) Break up the routine, go to Groupon or search on the Internet for something new to do with each other. There are usually hundreds of things to do in a major city, ranging from completely free, to a dollar, to hundreds of dollars or anywhere in between. You will probably see a bunch of things that you have never done before. You can go and explore them, which is going to keep your relationship fresh.

As you keep your relationship fresh this is going to make your marriage thrive instead of survive. I challenge you to do these actions and implement them in your life on a regular basis. If nothing else keep it fresh just to keep the fun going in your married life. Eventually you will start competing with each other to see who can come up with the most fun. You will thrive instead of survive.

CHAPTER 06

Growing Together

Adventure may hurt you, but monotony will kill you even faster especially in your marriage.

-Daniel Faust

So monotony, it's just something that dies inside. Why do I need to grow together? What benefits will I see if I improve along with my spouse? One of them is a lasting marriage. When you increase your personal development, you continue to get closer and closer to your partner. When a plant stops growing, it dies. When a person stops growing, they die. When a marriage is no longer evolving, a lasting relationship dies.

It also brings happiness, because if you see the beauty of your spouse or yourself growing, you observe it from a distance. Also, bringing oneness. As you grow together in Christ, you're on one edge, and your spouse is on the other, and as you grow together, you become one together. Another benefit, healthier living. As you grow together, you're going to become more balanced together. When you're in conflict, and you're not improving together, and everything is driving apart, it brings stress, and you're not healthy.

Also, the most important thing about growing together is intimacy. Intimacy is huge. It's 'into me see, ' and it constantly infusing in almost every element of marriage as we speak about it. As you grow together, your intimacy is going to grow together. It's a magnificent thing.

Your shocking fact for chapter 6, a study published February of this year in the Journal Psychoneuroendocrinology found that married couples have lower levels of stress hormone cortisol compared with single or divorced participants.

Elevated levels of cortisol can lead to inflammation, which contributes to various chronic ailments like heart disease. Welcome to being a male, you're already prevalent, and at least your marriage is helping you to get away from that. Diabetes and cancer researchers note. Take that fact with you, and you can look in that journal yourself if you want to research that, as of 2017 this is still prevalent. Even with the 'divorce rate' at 50%, which we talked about earlier, is a bunch of BS.

What's the contrast if we don't grow together? Our dream in our marriage is to develop together into a beautiful picture of the Gospel and for others to see God. When we allow monotony to set in, it damages not one, not two, but three relationships. What are you saying, Danny? I don't understand these three relationships?

In a Christian marriage, you have three relationships that get impacted in your interaction with your spouse. One is yours; one is your spouse's and also your relationship with God.

Those three relationships should be a part of all elements of your marriage. It especially hurts the most when we go over and not grow together.

Definition time: what's growing together or intimacy? It's a closeness of observation or knowledge of a subject. In marriage, this is your spouse, which shows you are into me see.

Intimacy, into me see.

How do I bring growing together and intimacy in a practical way in our marriage ?

Our first suggestion to you is reading a book together. That would be huge. As you read together, you find out the motives/values of your spouse which will help you grow . We recommended several publications such as the "Meaning of Marriage," by Dr. Timothy Keller and "Love and Respect," by Dr. Eggerichs. As you read these books together as a couple, you will grow together, because you'll start seeing things that you never understood before. I never realized this myself until I started this process. This experience can give you what Christ wants to change in you or reveal what Christ wants to change in your spouse. Then you each grow because you're actually on the path together. Just as simple as sharing this activity together.

Dividing into books together is huge. Hopefully the Bible is number one book in your relationship. Again, in our family we tend to struggle with that, so this is a challenge for us as it's a challenge to you. After you build in Bible time, then start reading a book together. If you both love reading, this is going to be easy for you. If one hates reading and the other one doesn't then it might be a minor challenge to do. If both of you hate reading, this is going to be a big challenge to you.

Here's some advice. You can do it one or two ways that we found that are helpful. One is if one person hates it, one person loves it, usually the person that loves it can read to the spouse that hates it. Typically, the non-reading spouse enjoys listening; they just don't like reading so that you can do that. That's one way of doing it.

Another way of doing it is audio books, In today's modern age, most books are available in audio format, find a good audio bible first to share together and then look for good audio books to share also. (This book will be audio in 2018)

And in the worst-case scenario, you both just hate reading; you can take devotions. Devotions are little books that you can read, and you can absorb that little bit of growth one step at a time because some people just can't digest Charles Spurgeon, some people need to take baby steps with a short little book like Our Daily Bread.

Choose whatever book's (paper, e-book, or audio)that works best for you. It will help you discover the motives, the values, and the personality style, which equals individual behavior & the character of that person that you're married to, This is your spouse in Christ.

This will help you guys grow together.

Another way to grow together and not allow monotony to set in is regular vacationing.

Wall Street actually posted an article about the benefits of vacationing and what Wall Street says is that vacationing can decrease depression, stress, make you live longer, healthier marriages, which makes people closer to their family. Also going on a regular vacation induces romance and very much helps you thrive in life. I know what you're saying right now, and I'm going to nip this objection right in the bud. You are probably thinking that you don't have the budget to vacation well. Can you buy Starbucks? If you buy Starbucks you're spending an average $5 a day, $25 a week, $100 a month, $1,200 a year and an average vacation can cost $1,200. From WorldVentures, Vacations2Go, Groupon, Armed Force Vacation club, to AirB2B there are multiple options with insane deals. Additionally if you are willing to vacation in off seasons (like Oct-May) you can go destinations over the world for pennies on the dollar. Lastly, if you barrier is the children, we understand that but I tell you even with children there is a myriad of options. If you get landlocked in making this happen, contact us and we will give you some workarounds for your situations. This is essential in life to unwind to recharge and grow together.

Love is about growing together as a couple, learning about each other, and not giving up

Regular vacation, often. Stay vacationed.

The last thing we want to give you is a how to grow together in intimacy is sharing hobbies together. What this does is shows love and appreciation to your spouse and you get to see a side of your spouse that you don't see in the hustle and bustle of life. If you're working shoulder to shoulder and back to back in life, you tend only to see the task-oriented side of that person. We have four unique personality styles, we have the dominant, the inspiring, the steady, and the conscientious. If we just stay in the hustle & bustle, we only show one side of the spectrum of who we are. For me, it's primarily dominance, and that's all my spouse sees most of the time, and my kids. If you see my wife in the hustle/bustle mode, she gets into the conscientious style, and it's all about quality, answers, excellence, and value.

That works for a season, but then you're going to be drained. That doesn't help us grow together, so we share a hobby together. An example is I(Daniel) went one-time zip lining, it showed a whole different side of my spouse, I never thought how adventurous she was and how scared and almost peeing my pants I was doing that same event.

But I took it on to share that hobby together, we bought a Go Pro and tried to tape it. I spun so many times, and we were going so fast that if I peed my pants, it would have been dry. Sharing your hobbies also will give you a new level of appreciation to your spouse. So get out of the hustle /bustle groove and share a hobby together.

It can be inside a house, outside a house, whatever you need. You're smart enough and capable enough to figure out how together. (If not, find us on social media and ask for suggestions)

Let's get into some of the objections.

Here is one for you, "It doesn't seem right to go somewhere I don't like" Sometimes we don't like something because of perceptions. I(Daniel) don't enjoy zip lining, but when I was with my wife I enjoyed the time and wouldn't trade the experience for anything We could think like roller coasters are scary and you hear that as a kid. Then you're like 25-35 years old. Roller coasters are intimidating; I'm never going to go on a rollercoaster. This can limit your opportunities in life. Lastly, if you can remember the foods that you hated as a kid and that you now like as an adult, this would be just like the same thing. I don't eat carrots; they look slimy. Over time your perception isn't going to change, and if you cook the food right, you're not going to eat it. So if the event is primed right, you might like it.

Give it time and perception, and it can change. If you're still not sure and you hate this, then go for the person. My friend Bill Myers did that one time It was my 25th birthday, he came to a birthday. We went to Dave & Buster's, Laser tag, and "The Cheesecake Factory". He came to this event because he loved me not the things that we were doing. That brought a smile on my face and it can brings a smile to your spouse's face, This type of sacrifice is worth more than jewels.

Maybe another objection you're having is the feeling that, 'change is so hard for me". Depending on your style, change might be easy or difficult. If you sit in the difficult camp, I would recommend making proactive changes. When you make a proactive change, you make it at your pace. If you wait until it is a reactive change it will be a lot more painful and quick. A lot of times in reactive changes, the consequences are typically not good. Reactive change is typical because of external motivators. We don't like proactive, (not the cleanser) because it's usually an internal motivator to make different choices. Internal motivation and introspection is hard If you take this step by step, you'll see the fruit rather than the collateral damage and the reactive stage.

Reactively acting out is never a good thing. Will you choose reactive or proactive?

"I want to grow together, but my spouse doesn't". Another objection you might be thinking. God allows our example of growth and change to be infectious over time. Even in the trials that are lengthy in time, when we are faithful to him, typically our marriage will be even better in five years or less. Dr. Timothy Keller talks about that in "The Meaning of Marriage". The most important growth in a marriage is your own. Let God use you as a light for your spouse to join you.

When (Michelle) worked on her healing from past brokenness it helped her immensely with emotional and spiritual battles. It took I(Daniel) two more years to jump on board and start the growing process but it was worth it. Our marriage looks like nothing it has before and it would have never been equipped to serve you all.

If you are struggling with this concept, find a married couple you trust to glean off because the only way they truly thrive is growing in Him.

So your three actions as the reader (I'm glad that you're still sticking through, you are halfway through the book) to take and apply.

1)Choose another marriage book together to read after this one, because this only covers broad strokes for you to start the journey. We want to dive deep in your marriage and there are many more resources. Listed below are our suggestions:

Real Marriage (Mark Driscoll);

The Meaning of Marriage (Timothy Keller),

Love and Respect, Cracking the Communication Code(Dr. Eggerichs).

If you need additional recommendations, find us on "Learn and Live" via Facebook and ask us what marriage recommendation books or find us personally on Facebook,

2) Set a time to sit down and plan a vacation together. When you sit down and plan use "and" statements, rather than "but" statements. The use of "and" it your sentences brings positivity, while the use of "but" brings negativity. We recommend WorldVentures when you shop for vacations. You can budget your stay into your paycheck rather than cram it into summer budget. Our main goal for you is to vacation well.

3) Lastly, go to your local city website and look for a list of events, hobbies, classes to take together. See if you can find something you both can enjoy or let one choose one and then go with them and remember to bring a positive attitude with you. Bring a smile with you. Smiles are infectious. This infectious feeling is called "mirror neurons". When you send out positive body language, the person that sees you is going to tend to send back the same positive body language. It's going to bring happiness back and forth, at least for the short term until you come to joy.

As you're going into the next chapter, remember that growing together is going to help you thrive together, to break up the monotony and to keep your marriage thriving instead of surviving.

Join us in chapter 7, thanks.

CHAPTER 07

Happiness Scale

Happiness is fleeting. In marriage, the real goal is to find joy, which will fulfill us and the entire cycle of marriage. Once joy is found, you will thrive.

-MICHELLE FAUST

Happiness, marital satisfaction is a thing that we want to achieve. What benefits does this goal bring to you? What does it provide to your spouse?

Number one, it lowers your stress, usually when you're happy you're not stressed. Happiness doesn't cause stress or a heart attack. Also as you're happy, you're more productive at work. When you are happy. You are more productive at home and work. The saying "Happy wife, Happy life" has some truth to it. Very little work at home or work gets done when you are angry. You might as well keep your marital satisfaction; your happiness up so you can be more productive at work & home.

Happiness is contagious – because as you're happy, other people want to be satisfied. Happiness over an extended period is joy, so it's infectious over time. Even the angry people will be like, "Why are you so happy?" Over time, they want to have what you have. As you're comfortable at home and satisfied with your marriage, you can bring it to work and be contagious for others.

Also, happiness brings resiliency, because if you can be happy through the times of trial in your marriage, you're going to be more resilient, be able to take a beating when it happens, and thrive even in that. Trials will come so find your happiness to thrive in any season.

My wife, my twins, and my daughter almost died, all in a matter of like a 2-3 year period. If I had a better happiness, I wouldn't have had as much stress and been more resilient dealing with those situations. It's entirely changed from year 2-4 until now, and I think I'm a lot more resilient (we almost became homeless three times). God's been working alot in us, We want to grow in resilience and perseverance so we can be a testimony for him and to you guys.

Another thing, it increases communication. People talk a lot more when they are happy, not so much when you are furious. That typically doesn't happen. Usually, when you're glad, you're thriving, you want to talk more, which increases your increase communication.

Time for our shocking fact or statistic. Boredom with your spouse or your happiness scale is one of the top 10 reasons for divorce across all marriage studies. This information is provided by couplescounselingchicago.net.

What's the contrast? What's the pain? We can live about 40 days without food, three days without water, 5 minutes without oxygen and only a moment without joy. It is essential to infuse into our lives & marriage. Typically without pleasure there's sadness, sadness leads to depression, depression leads to health issues, and it eventually takes us out/saps our lives. We should be looking for happiness that leads to joy.

What does that mean? We're talking about a happiness scale, which is overall marital satisfaction. Marital satisfaction is a particular case of relationship satisfaction. (Hopefully, you're having that too and if not, use this book as a benchmark), and it is the degree to which partners in marriage assess their approval of different aspects of the marital relationships.

That's a pretty colossal definition. Let's jump into the "how to's" of martial satisfaction and to keep it high.

First off, we need to deal with the unspoken expectations. Typically, this is more in the early parts of marriage and as we walk into different parts of life that we have not discussed/experienced. Unspoken expectations are holding someone to your ideas and never telling them. As we talked about earlier, the cups up versus the cups down story. This was a standard that I was not aware of initially when we were dating. This didn't come up until we moved as a married couple. That would be an unspoken expectation. When I started seeing the cups down, I put them up, we never spoke, we got into arguments about it, and that was one of the unspoken expectations. Another one for me was my household standards. I had to start saying, hey, here's the household standards, but it was more my household standards; so that caused more division and not satisfaction.

From sex to houseguest, we all have a lot of unspoken expectations. In premarital counseling you deal with some of these but not all. For you all to keep the martial satisfaction up, I would suggest weekly to have "coffee chats" on some of your expectations in key areas. After that, you need to come to uniform agreement on how to live this out. It needs to be unbiased and bathed in prayer for the expectation. A lot of times, one submits while the other person gets there way. If this happens, an underlying bitterness can happen and ruin martial satisfaction. Work on regularly because it is like foxes in a vineyard. It will destroy it over time.

Another thing you can do to keep marital satisfaction and happiness is prioritizing. When we put priorities in the wrong order, this can suck joy away. This situation requires that you and your spouse separately to have a conversation with God. Then come together on your prioritizing. An example is if you put your kids first via their love and affection, your spouse is typically going to get forgotten. If you put your kids first, you lose your spouse. The same holds true if you put your job/business/career over your spouse. Any other order than God>Spouse>Kids>Friends is a recipe for disaster. That's where the priorities should be. You're doing the job to take care of the wife and the kids, but if the work becomes the sole thing, you lose wife and kids.

Joy does not simply happen to us. We have to choose joy and keep choosing it every day

Henri J. M. Nouwen

Our last "how to" is to learn to communicate your spouse's love languages. Dr. Gary Chapman teaches on the love language, so I'm going to give you a quick summary. You can also go to Learn and Live on Facebook to watch the little videos, but I'm going to now give you a quick synopsis of what they are.

Physical touch:, you're going to communicate this by hugs, kisses, holding hands, things of that nature, rubbing of the back, rubbing of feet, like massages, having your hair played with, things of that nature. You like to give it; you want to receive it. If your spouse is physical touch, do those things on a regular basis, do it with the right emotional heart.

Words of affirmation: If you or your spouse are words of affirmation, here are some examples: I want to hear that you love me, appreciate me, enjoy me, and honor me. Even comments that you say in the bedroom, you're a sex goddess, those things are words of affirmation, to show your spouse that you love them.

(Disclaimer: Physical touch and word of affirmation can be displayed inside and outside of bedroom. For more specifics, please read "the Five Love languages by Dr Gary Chapman)

Gifts: it's pretty simple. A person likes gifts and it's not because they're prideful and materialistic, it's the surprise, they like to open up things, they like to have small gifts. You're going to have to learn about them and the types of gifts they want so you can serve them.

They usually like giving gifts, and they typically enjoy receiving them. All these languages, they want to give and to receive. That's how you know. They're saying; you just haven't hugged me in a long time; they lack physical touch as their love language. Like you haven't talked to me in a long time, you haven't affirmed me X information. I just wish I would have somebody to give me something, to get excited by some gifts.

Next one, acts of service, which is mine specifically; they like to do acts of service for their spouse or their loved ones. They love to do specific things or get particular jobs done. For example, acts of service for me let me sleep in on Father's Day. It took me ten years to finally receive that gift from my family. That was huge for my wife and my kids! If they want to do that on a monthly basis, get the house picked up, go over and get a task done that I don't want to get done or let me sleep in, or putting something together which I hate doing, acts of service. Huge.

Then the last love language is quality time. This person wants to have a shared activity and shared time together, usually face-to-face. There are many different dialects of each of these languages; you'll have to figure out the nuances for you.

Learn these love languages; there's a book by Dr. Gary Chapman, the Five Love Languages. There's also a military version of his book, appreciation, apology languages. He's written many excellent books; I got to meet him in person, I'm able to have occasional text message conversations with him, it's been a great blessing. We're hoping he endorses the book, so when he magically stumbles on this, maybe he'll do that. But if not, he's a great man of God and we're thankful to learn the communication love languages.

Let's jump into our objections, because by this point now you're like, that's a lot of information.

Maybe objection 1 is I can never make them happy. I would consider that valid. We can't decide on how people will react, but we all will whisper or scream if joy is lacking. You and I can be a conduit to serve in this capacity. Love tanks fill as we honor our spouses. Don't make the justification that your spouse's love tank needs to be filled solely by Jesus. I did that early in our marriage, and that was a massive devastation, which I continue to work through. Thankfully a lot of things have changed, but a lot of my words sometimes bite me in the butt.

Knowing someone's unspoken expectations is impossible. How am I supposed to know all their implicit expectations? If we take the time to observe our spouse, which is an active process, we can discover those expectations. Not all of them, but ones over time. We can also ask them flat out or after we've gone through conflict. Obviously gone through disagreements, find a safe place to ask flat out, hey I observed this, is this an expectation of yours? This would need to be an agreed process if you do it after conflict to add to your conflict resolution. It is possible, and it will take time, but it's so worth it, going over and understanding those unspoken expectations.

Take delight in the Lord and he will give you the desires of your heart

Psalm 37.4 NIV

The last one, we are so different in priorities and can't be on the same page. Just as you change the way you prioritize for hygiene in the morning, when you first got married you're like, hey I need to coordinate my spit actions, I might take a shower now in the morning instead of the evening. Our bigger priorities can change to align. To achieve this will require longer and be more conversations, but it's possible.

We, my wife and I, tend to put ourselves under the same authority regarding where we get teaching, which helps us realign our priorities. That would be huge too, to where you put your preferences at, is getting good teaching, the same lesson across the board. You can't always be there every single Sunday, especially if you're a traveling man like me, but whenever you get a chance, it also grows the relationship.

Your three actions as a reader today you should take as a result of reading this chapter:

1) Challenge you to read the Tyranny of Urgency by Charles Hummel, a small book that will expand on priorities.

2) Learn your love languages. There is a love language for you that Dr. Gary Chapman's ministry supports. That might be a fast-tracked way or do it by the books. Do it this week so that you can serve your spouse in one tangible way in their love language. Just one, not 10,000.

3) As you're getting your weekly dates, plan one date a month to discuss your observations on your spouse. Unspoken expectations. When you both agree to discovery, ask how you can meet their expectation, as long as it's a healthy way.

As we close this chapter of the happiness scale, we want your marriages to thrive in the many different ways. Happiness, which leads to joy, is going to be one that's going to last not just temporary, but especially if it's the joy of Christ, it's going to be an eternity.

Check you in the next one.

CHAPTER 08

Beyond Limitations

Brokenness is like a fog that can just roll over us. It can limit us, except for one thing that is missing: hope. Hope brings healing much like the sun burns the fog away. Bring on the sun.

-Daniel Faust

Beyond limitations is talking about brokenness, how to get through it and be set free. When you're free from brokenness, there is five specific benefits or pleasures that you can experience.

First is restoration. As you're free from brokenness, you're restored to who God made you. I am now in Christ in Daniel Faust or Christ in Michelle Faust or as my pastor friend says, Christ in John Lynch. (Insert your name) You are restored.

As you are restored, you also get freedom. Freedom from the bonds, shackles and the limitations that impeded you. Sometimes it has been so long that you didn't know you were held captive.

It also brings back control, because now we're not under the control of brokenness and it's us that are back in control. We're able to allow the Holy Spirit to control us, which also leads to peace, which peace is enormous because it passes all understanding, which leads finally into joy as we talked about earlier. Do you want joy?

When we get to joy, we can be free in him no matter the circumstances. We want for you in your marriage. To be free from the bondage of sin, brokenness and death. This happens when you not allow limitations to hold you captive any longer

Our shocking fact or statistic I learned when I was dealing with mental health/sexual assault world, is that 1 out of every 7 people has experienced sexual abuse in some form. You can walk into any office, church, or grocery store and find sexual assaults victims. For every 70 people in that grocery store/church/office, 10 of them have gone through some type of sexual abuse. This is just one form of brokenness.

What is contrast if we don't deal with the pain, addictions, past hurts, and the abuse? Your divorce increase to 90%. Yes, 90% Let that soak in for a moment.... I used to work in mental health and actually saw this on a regular basis. There is hope even in these odds, so let's figure that out.

What are limitations? What is our definition so we can get into the how's of how to deal with that? Limitations are factors that can affect mental satisfaction; this can include past hurts, abuse, addictions, which in turn create barriers preventing openness and freedom. (Michelle Faust)

How do we deal with limitations? How do we deal with the brokenness? How do we deal with the barriers, how do we deal with the past hurts, abuse and addictions, which can turn into obstacles, so we're not open and not free?

1) First is corporate prayer. This concept is probably foreign to you if it's the first time you've read this type of book and/or you're not a Christian. As a Christian couple, it still might be foreign to you as you don't do it on a regular basis, but I highly recommend it. (We need it to) We are learning and living together.

When you pray for each other and with each other God moves. It causes us to be unified; it also promotes emotional intimacy, invites God into the relationship and even changes our individual and our corporate bonds. I believe most time this is why Christian marriages split because if we're not praying together, we can't stay together.

The formula for broken relationships: it starts out face to face, and we're getting involved in the word in prayer and relationships. We're regular date nights, and then we go shoulder to shoulder, going over and working together side by side, which works well in some things, but not in marriages and long-term situations. Then we go back to back, and apparently, we're not praying for each other and not having corporate prayer. When we are back to back, I'll pray for myself, you pray for yourself, and we'll just go over and deal with each other's stuff only when triage moments hit, (Not a good thing) Then we just walk away(emotional, spiritually, and sometimes practically), and by the time we turn back to look at each other we're like, "Who the hell are you? You're not my friend". Finally we split ways in form of a divorce, adultery, co-habituating together but not living married life together.

Cooperate prayer one way to help break those limitations, break those past hurts and addictions.

After implementing corporate prayer then you can devotions to your arsenal. (If you do this separately, then it won't be as effective)

Devotions are books that you can buy usually through Christian bookstores, Wal-Mart, or Barnes & Noble to put our spiritual minds in sync. There are daily, monthly, morning or evening, online, or apps for devotions. A couple good writers of devotions are Charles Spurgeon, Oswald Chambers, or your local pastor can give you recommendations. Devotions empower us to get into God's word, and it begins to ask questions, questions we would never ask ourselves, items we would never ask our spouse, questions that God would pray for us to answer for ourselves.

Devotions will helps you grow; it's going to stretch you, challenge you, it's going to put you more together to break those past hurts It's going to ask you about those previous hurts differently. It's going to deal with your abuse, your addiction in his way. It's going to convict you to change, to work through those past hurts/abuse/ and dependencies in a way only God can. When this happens, you can become free from those barriers to be open and free.

After you go through corporate prayer and devotions, then you can add small groups/ community groups to your arsenal. Community groups are small groups that meet during the week via the local church's oversight. They're like-minded people in your church that will either discuss a topic out the Bible or a topic that pastor spoke on the prior week. Usually, those community group/small group leaders will then go over pre-written questions. Within this group you can connect with other couples who can help you grow your marriage. Sometimes seeing a couple going through the same trials as you have helps you stay in the battle. This type of safe group will help you thrive.

(Disclaimer: When selecting a community/small group, get into prayer and devotional time to ensure you are choosing the group best for both of you. Sometimes a longer commute is worth the safety/security of your spiritual walk)

With those three things addressed, and if you still need a more in-depth help, I would recommend Celebrate Recovery. These particular groups meet across the nation, (Google "Celebrate Recovery" to find the closest one to you). It's like "12 steps" for Christians. It usually goes through codependency, anger, sexual trauma, alcohol and drug abuse, etc.

We went through "Celebrate Recovery" a couple seasons ago,. When we were in Arkansas, we orginaly thought we were down there to start our business and ministry.
It so happens that this decision we made God used for us to get some healing. I started to see issues of that decision reflecting on my wife and I. For us, we both started going to "Celebrate Recovery". We didn't stay that long, but for the few months we were there, it was very much useful. I still reflect on that today on how angry of a person I was. My wife can tell you more about her stuff if she wants to afterward. It helped us to get through the trials, to grow, break thru the limitations, and start the healing process. We didn't overcome all of them, but we started to get away from the shackles of the past hurts and abuse. We recommend going to Celebrate Recovery.

For the law of the Spirit of life has set you free in Christ Jesus from the law of sin and death

Romans 8:2

Another more intense and private option to utilize in the battle of limitation u can to a consultant, coach, or counselor. This people are usually detached from the situation and will give great advice, strategies or prayer to deal with these limitations. You would call one these people typically when situations are affecting your daily life and impacting others. I would recommend to not wait until you are pondering divorce or worse heading down the track of depression or suicide. Preventive maintenance is always better than damage control.

When you are making the decision between a coach, consultant, and counselor you need to understand the difference. (the following definitions come from http://doctorgresham.com/the-difference-between-coaching-consulting-counseling-and-psychotherapy/) Coaching is about setting and achieving goals with the assistance of a person who asks you helpful and focused questions. Your coach's emphasis is on your strengths, weaknesses, opportunities and challenges related to the goals you have set. Consulting is the service you seek to answer a specific problem using the expert knowledge of a professional. A consultant has specialized knowledge and expertise on the process or the problem that is of interest to you. Often a consultation will be a short term engagement on one specific topic. Consultants work with individuals, families, groups and organizations. Occasionally teaching or training will be part of the engagement. Counseling is the process that focuses on the relief of distress. Your counselor should be someone with whom you can build trust and openness. You and your counselor will work together to help you cope, adapt and build skills to reduce distress.

It takes an average of 10 years to go "I to "We" in marriage If there are any brokenness (abuse, rape, etc) add another decade on the clock.

Together you and your counselor may look at patterns in your life to help you come to a greater understanding of yourself and build newer more adaptive methods of coping. The relationship will be most helpful if your counselor is warm, accepting and authentic. Additionally, you usually have to have a medical diagnosis when it's marriage counseling, one or another spouse has got to have a mental health diagnosis. If not, in 12 sessions they're done with you, because they're usually taking third party insurance. Some counselors take payments but range from 150-300 a hour.

We hope this equips you in making good decisions on breaking thru these limitations to thrive in your marriage

Today in this particular chapter, Beyond Limitations, you only getting two actions for you the reader to take on because we seriously want you to implement this into your daily life. If we had to choose anything for you to immediate apply in your life, these two would be crucial to add to your daily life.

1) Set a day to pray with your spouse. Start with something small and grow from there. You can say, Lord I thank you for my spouse, thank you that I can get home and didn't die today, Amen. Once you implement daily prayer you should implement corporate prayer. One way to do this with ease is prayer through the scripture with your spouse. An example is as you read "Psalms 25" aloud, you take a moment after reading a few versesand pray about the truths exposed in those verses. Sometimes you can only be thanking God in this method of prayer and other times depending on the context you can try to tie your prayers to God and your spouse. (Thanking God for my spouse's faithfulness to sticking through the good/bad of our marriage)

2) Our second challenge to is to get into a devotion on a regular basis. As we suggested above, there are several types, locations, and ways to get a devotion. From reading to listening during your commute. This will help you get into the practice of getting time with God to reorient your mind towards him. Once you establish your own personal devotion, then ask your spouse to see about integrating a couple devotion on a regular basis. I would recommend a sit down discussion on scheduling time, place, frequency, book, etc. Each season of life can increase or decrease the frequency but consistency and buy-in is most important.

Those are your two actions that you should take as a result of reading this chapter. We want to go over and pray for you guys, to get beyond these limitations. Dear Heavenly Father, we ask for each couple that is reading this book to become free of their brokenness, to be restored, to have freedom, bring back control, have that inner peace that you want to give. You want us to have joy. When sin came to the world, it bought limitations to our live. You didn't leave us there. You brought you Son Jesus to die for us to break us free from sin and these limitations. We ask for these couples strength to intergrate you into their lives from them to thrive in their marriage, have a legacy, and to serve you calling in their lifes. Thank you for this couple and pray that through you we can serve and love them. In the mighty name of Jesus Chirst. Amen!

See you in Chapter 9, Under the Sheets.

CHAPTER 09

Under the Sheets

Sex. God, gross, or gift?

-Pastor Mark Driscoll.

Where do you sit in this equation? We want to help you with your sexual compatibility in your life. You probably thinking "What is that and what do you mean there are benefits?" Yes, there is sexual combability and once you learn these principles you can thrive in the bedroom. (You probably been waiting for this chapter or you skipped directly to this chapter. Ha-ha you been caught lol)

Well the first benefit is that procreation increases, which is cool. You get to have excellent little versions of yourself. Next, a deeper intimacy builds that brings you 'into me see' Then, when you're sexually compatible under the sheets it brings companionship. It brings friendship to a whole new level when you're sexually compatible. Also it brings a deeper physical pleasure. One of God's greatest gift he gives to us is sex, which is an excellent pleasure. Lastly, it takes away shame and sin. When sex is done right, done under God's eyes, and goes over to serve that person, there's no shame and no sin in this beautiful privilege.

Here is your shocking fact or statistic: (I was shocked),61% of relationships from Christianitytoday.com think they need to try sex before they get married, and then they separate sex from their Christianity. When you add co-habitation, you are pushing a divorce factor of 60%.

What's the contrast? When sex is a god, it is the primary focus, which can add shame, pornography, and sin. When sex is gross, we limit or avoid sex altogether, unless for procreation, which denies the blessing that God gave us, so we want to have sex as a gift.

What is sexual compatibility in your life? The definition of sexual compatibility is the extent to which a couple perceives their shared beliefs, preferences, desires and needs with their partner.

How do we understand sexual compatibility? We jump into the DISC model of behavior again and the reference for this paraphrased, is Body and Soul. (If you want to jump in deeper in this topic after this chapter, go to our resources page and find this book. It is a great read)

First, we're going to get into the dominant style. If you resonated with that direct, demander type of style, this is how you look at sex in a nutshell, and we only grab the essential nuggets that we thought would be worthwhile for you. If you're the dominant style, sex to them is a self-focused personal goal used to relieve frustration. Romance escapes them. Naturally, they like control and to make decisions for others. They need to know what's going on and fast. They can use anger to control a situation and can use conflict to control the room. Foreplay is little if none. If you're a dominant female, the dominance can be perceived as 'the time of the month' if you know what I mean. They like varied activities, and sex is a conquest for them. If being a great lover is their goal, then you'll be wowed, and your socks will fly off.

(Disclaimer: As we're talking about these personal sexual compatibility styles, these are the extreme natures/out of control of the Holy Spirit typically. It can come off a little bit negative. Just be aware of that. And it's not saying it's a bad thing, all these styles are a good thing when under control of the Holy Spirit).

Our next style is the I, the "inspiring" style. For this type, sex will be great for you because the person doesn't want rejection. They will try creative things to please their spouse. As their spouse, you'll need to be open to communicate about their sexual desires, needs, and expressions. They like to do it, and they want you to do the same. Sex between two high "I" spouses will be superior, but sometimes they might forget about sex due to the excellent communication. You might have that tremendous emotional/physical connection and then lose interest in sex.

They were both naked, the man and his wife, and were not ashamed

GENESIS 2.25

Their emotional need to receive praise is especially needed in the bedroom, so definitely give them verbal praise. The more vocal you are during intimacy the better. If you have conflict in the bedroom, this person will use the win-win technique to work things out. They want things to work out; they don't want to have conflict especially in the bedroom. High I females have a deep need to talk and to relate to promote intimacy in the bedroom. So, guys if you're with a high I female, don't expect to be like wham bam thank you, ma'am. It's just not going to flow that well.

Their views on sex are to wow you in performance, words, and touch to make you feel fantastic. Especially men do this, men will want to wow you in performance, words, and touch. For the ladies in this style, they need the communication, the emotional and relational connection to spark great sex. They will not have problems expressing their feelings and desires either; they will tell you exactly what they are looking for if this is their primary style.

Our next style is the "S" the supportive lover. They look for security, trust, and commitment to satisfying sex. It is the foundation for them. They will be constant and reserved, they don't expect much experimentation naturally. They're not going to be like, "let's go hang off the chandelier and get our freak happening". No, they're not going to do that naturally. Over time, maybe so. S's are passionate, but the mood is imperative, so you've got to make sure that the atmosphere is right and that they're in the right mood. The longer the relationship, the better the sex. It's like wine; it gets better with age. If the situation is right for them, intimacy is on. They're not much for change in intimacy patterns, so they're like, "let's do it this way, consistent, enjoyable, not too much wanting to try something different". Intimacy builds throughout the day and trust is critical for them.

You could have a 9.5 out of 10 on the "spouse sex scale, and you can blow it anytime. The sexual trust account is build it throughout the day, and trust is critical to them. You want to affirm them in the small and the significant things that they do, inside and outside the bedroom. It will pay dividends. Also, they will be the most sacrificial in the bedroom, even if they're not in the mood, Their goal is to serve.

I know for myself, I've seen this in my marriage that my spouse will serve because we know that sexual moods are not always at the same time. We can do everything right and sometimes we are not there, and this quality shows their servant heart. We are glad for the supportive style in that realm. We can glean from all the types.

Lastly and certainly not the least, the conscientious lover. They will be very technical and pointed on performing well. The emotional aspect can be put on the back burner. If they make suggestions, it will be very detailed and not look at the sensitive side of the talk. For example, "You need to raise your leg at a 47.5-degree angle," not considering that you just broke your leg yesterday. If disapproval is pointed out, they will become withdrawn and silent. They can be gravely wounded by disapproval, and measure their self-worth as lovers by performance. If they're balanced, you will receive excellent sex in all the realms. You get the technical stuff, you get the emotional stuff, and everything just flows like a perfect symphony. As they go through the day, commitment is enormous to them. You've got to keep that in mind. For example, you said, "I'm going to bring flowers home", then you better do it. If not, this will reflect "Under the Sheets" as withdrawal. They are slow movers ensure DEOR (Desire, Excitement, Orgasm, Release). They are excellent performers in execution. Don't expect them to be like wham/bam/thank you, ma'am. They enjoy encouragement in this regard and rebuking in a non-threatening way.

If you're concerned about their performance, you want to deliver the concern in a friendly, nonthreatening way. Recommendations are key for change in this regard. They are great lovers that meet desires/wants that are clear to them. Not clear to you, clear to them. Give them the right environment and you'll see an incredible love and warmth and see their creativity is thoroughly structured.

The sexual intimacy section was probably the chapter that you wanted to receive the most amount of information. (for more info" Go to our "Resources page, our store link, and "google" Body & Soul) Now let's dive into some objectives.

1) "How would I find these answers? It is intimidating to ask". As we stated earlier, you can read "Body & Soul" and ask these observation via a question in an inquisitive way. An example would be" May I read a description to you and tell me if this resonates with you?" You can experiment this trying the different styles or for our cautious people you can buy a personality profile to validate the information to your spouse. (this would be the safest way)

By night on my bed I sought him whom my soul loveth

Song of Solomen 3:1 KJV

2)" Is this valid? Why do I need to know this?" The DISC model behavior has been around since 1926 by Dr. William Marston Also, millions of people have taken these assessments with an 80-90% accuracy. I've been a behavioral consultant myself for six years, and every profile I usually given has an 80-90% accuracy. It's very rare when I have one and think, wow, this is way off from your displayed style. Lastly, this information is not just for "Under the Sheets", but for any relationship, you come to meet. The sexual personality style is just one element of the DISC model of Human Behavior.

3) "What if my spouse doesn't fit into these categories?" These are broad strokes that we are visiting to get you a baseline into sexual personality styles. This topic is probably new/foreign for you, we didn't want to overwhelm you. If you 're wanting to get specific info for yourself or your spouse, we recommend a personality assessment and a consultation, because there's not a sexual personality profile yet. (If there is a demand, we will work on it) From there, we can contextualize to you and your spouse.

Challenge time!!!

1) Let's say you got tempted by this chapter in a right way, and you want to know more about how to get under the sheets efficiently. If you're going to dive more into the covers, go read Body and Soul, (Resources page, our store link, then search for book) Want to "SCUBA Dive" into this topic, schedule aa consultation.

2) Head to our store (Resources page, our store link) and search for "four free lessons to better relationships". This will expound your knowledge on your spouse primary sexual, communication, and several other behavioral styles.

3)Take these tips and make a time to discuss your sexual-style with your spouse. You just don't do this over the dinner table, you have to plan it out. Discuss this s you're planning your date night, planning your devotions, planning your time together, your shared activities, things of this nature. Plan that time and say, hey, we're going out to date night this week, I want to discuss our sexual-styles, and maybe we can visit those sexual methods after we have our date night. Then take the knowledge and experiment with it. Take your time in the bedroom from toleration to acceptance or from acceptance to celebration. When you love your spouse, and learn how you each respond to the other's preferences, your sex life thrives which in turn start to make your marriage thrive.

That is a nutshell of understanding your sexual personality styles "Under the Sheets". We hope that this helps you in your growth and intimacy.

See you in next chapter.

CHAPTER 10

Unlocking You

Communication and Trust are two main ingredients for a successful relationship

-Unknown

The most significant blessing you can bring to your marriage is understandings yourself. When this happens, you can love your spouse with his love.

Understanding and unlocking yourself is the most important thing you can do in your life, and Tthere are actually five benefits I saw c, especially coming back from my deployment in 2007, This which actually helped my marriage to go from surviving to now thriving ten years later.

One of the benefits is operating in your strength. Instead of wasting your time to try to be everything to everybody, you get to work on your abilities to show your spouse who you are. Next, it helps you find your mission in life. Everyone asks you "What do you want to be when you grow up?" Some of us are in our 30's -60's still hunting for this answer. When you understand yourself and where your gifts lie, then you can find your mission that God has for you. Then, it helps you avoid pitfalls, because if you understand yourself, you're going to see your strengths and your weaknesses and what areas you're going to encounter. An example would be, I (Daniel) tend to bring up the past into a present situation on a regular basis. I can avoid that pitfall if I am aware of it. Rather than our spouses revealing this issue, we can be aware of those things and avoid that pitfall. Additionally, you can bring a broader intimacy into your relationship. No more needing to perform and put on a mask (trying to be somebody else). You're being who God has designed you to be. Lastly, you get to appreciate others including your spouse. When you become "unlocked" it frees you to receive love but also it frees you to give love. When we are locked up, we tend to be hurt and only deliver hurt in return. This unlocking of yourself breaks this cycle of being hurt and start receiving love. This overflow of love pours into others which you spouse can receive the first fruits of.

The words of the reckless pierce like swords, but the tongue of the wise brings healing

Proverbs 12:18

Shocking truth: The number one destroyer of marriages is communication, which when you break it down it's not knowing yourself.(Being "locked" up)

So what's the contrast of not "unlocking" ourselves? For years, I know only a glimmer of myself. Even the best of us only sees 50%(Jahara Windows). When I brought this 50% to my marriage via my tongue/wisdom it almost destroyed my marriage. We really need to dive into getting to know ourselves so we can thrive and not just survive. When you just survive too long, then eventually something dies. What will die on your watch?

What's our secret definition of unlocking you? Unlocking you is in essence "Wisdom", which according to Webster's dictionary is "the ability to discern inner qualities and relationships". You're learning to recognize yourself and the interactions you display to others. When you learn to understand yourself, you can learn to appreciate others. In essence, if I know you and you know me, then we can have a better relationship. So how do we do that?

Let's get right into the three how's.

1) We have motives. These are the 'why' to what we do. From the "why" we put glasses in the cabinet down to "why" we stay in the relationships we do. We need to understand the "why" in what we do. When we don't, we will just keep "shooting in the dark" and hope to hit the bullseye. Typically this is a "hit or miss" game. Especially in our close relationships, we don't want to play this dangerous game.

You're not going to understand absolutely everything of the "whys" but let take a page out of two wisest men of all time playbook. First, was Solomon. He was the richest man on earth and even he studied himself, humanity, and God to thrive as much as possible. Second, we have Jesus. He is our best example. Even the God of the universe grew in "wisdom", stature, and favor with God and man. If these two men invested into "Unlocking" themselves, we should be running towards "wisdom".

When you get married, your motives infuse into the marriage in a passive way. What do I mean by that? This happens when they get bumped by our spouse, as we seen from our example of the cup up, cup down issue from a couple of chapters ago, I would have never known what I valued on having the cups up compared to the cups down. This same theory holds true in your communication style, decision making, sexual preferences, etc.

I didn't realize how many problems I'm bumping into via other relationships because they're not as close to me. They just tolerated or eliminated me in a passive way. Our spouses shouldn't have to tolerate us, we need to challenge ourselves in our motives. When we find out our motives, then we see if this is "locking" ourselves up. If so we need to change it, to be "unlocked" and free. If it is a good motive and we share it our spouses, they have a great opportunity to understand and love you better. Lastly most of our motives are not worth dying for. Take the time to figure out the "why" to what you do, but don't go over and die for it. We tend to mix that up on a regular basis.

2) To go deeper in "unlocking you" is to learn about our values/ beliefs. Our beliefs are more deeply rooted, which can stand for our moral code. We have a specific moral code like, "Hey, I'm against murder." (Name your value, name your belief.) This element of our person should be the things that we're standing on/willing to die for. Let's go back to the laundry argument, when I had the discussion with my wife about laundry I was taking it too far. I made it a value/ belief that washing the clothing should be done in a certain way. Those extremes will kill you when you're taking something that's not even a true belief. It's probably just a preference. We definitely need to say, "Do I take something that's a preference and make it a value/belief. When you're going to do that, you're deciding to die for it. If this value/belief worth losing the person in front of you These conversations are better to have planned than impromptu. As a individual and a couple, I would recommend coming together to choose your values/beliefs together. When you are united on a value, you thrive together. If you divided on

a value, you die together.

3) Take time to understand your personality. You can start by rereading Chapter 2 and 9 to answer the two basic questions to see you baseline personality style. This is just the beginning to truly "unlock" you. Here is just one example that will open your eyes immensely

There's actually two different styles, (we didn't get into it in the beginning chapters, because we just didn't want to overwhelm you) You have a baseline "God" personality style and then you have an "Environmental" style. Your baseline style is at home with your spouse, with your kids, with your parents, with your really close friends. This style same the same because you feel "safe" being the real you. Then you have your environmental style which your coworkers, people you meet on the street see. This style adjusts to those people that you are interaction. Obviously if you naturally dominant at home, you might not bring that to work because that might not be deemed valuable. So you could display a more submissive style to not ruffle feathers.

> *Communication and Trust are two main ingredients for a successful relationship*
>
> -Unknown

When we understand this about ourselves, it going reduce the conflicts down 10-90%.

This was huge for me on my deployment, this was why this book is being written, this is why I want to share this with you.

As you're listening you might have some objections so let's bring them to the table.

1) Maybe this is you. "I know myself pretty well, and I've heard this several times. What is the point of learning this?" I've been a behavioral consultant for six years and I am still learning about myself. Like we discussed earlier, the average person can only see 50% of themselves at best. If you are still on the fence ask yourself: "How many conflicts have you had in the past month? Past week? Past year?" Conflicts are a "when" not an "if" so why not learn yourself well to "fight well"

2) This next one might fit a lot of you: "I have the God of the Bible, I have Jesus Christ, and that is enough." Scripture tells us that Jesus grew in wisdom, stature, and favor with God and man.(Luke 2:52) If the king of the universe was learning, we should follow our master's example. Additionally, as we look a biblical marriage of loving our wives and submitting to our husbands, (Ephesians 5:22-33) How do we do that practically within growing in wisdom of ourselves and them? I am telling you from experience in my marriage and seeing others that if you only love God or others, you marriage is on a slippery slope. Grow in Jesus, yourself, and others to thrive in this life and the next.

3) Lastly, another objection "This is only for work relationships and doesn't affect me. I do these personality things at work. They might work for a little bit, but at home, it never works." Have you ever had a work relationship spill into the house or vice versa? If so, you are wired to have relationships. Any relationship can spill into another, but the most significant relationship on the planet is called marriage. This relationship affects us the most regarding work-related effectiveness.. If you have a problem with Bob at work it might affect you at home but if you have a problem with your wife Susie, it's going to pour into your work. It will typically take over your thoughts. We have 70,000 ideas a

day. When we're usually in conflict, we tend to repeat those "tapes". You want to take these skills and bring them home.

Your three actions as the reader that we would like for you and you should take as a result of reading this chapter:

1) Schedule a personality consultation with us to help you understand yourself well. We can help you grow, it helps us improve, we learn and live together, and that is our calling, we want you to thrive.

2) Go to our Resources page to glean as much as you can of additional book we recommend. It has changed us so much to understand the "why" what we do. This info saved our marriage. Why not yours?

3) Lastly and most importantly is to meditate in Psalms and Proverbs to gain the best wisdom of yourself and Him. This place is always practical and relevant no matter where you are in life or stage you are in your Bible reading

Ten chapters down and 2 to go, hope you can stick it out with us and join us in Chapter 11. God bless you & see you in 11.

CHAPTER 11

Doctorate Degree

Being known is the bricks, being connected is the cement

-ANSHAR MARTIN

We invest in education to be experts in our field, which just lasts a fleeting moment, but getting a doctorate in your spouse lasts a lifetime.

I love this chapter!!! I heard this comment one time that "You need to get a doctorate in your spouse". This is something we all need to do. As your "marriage consultants" we will help you earn your "doctorate" in your spouse. This will be the best info in our "quiver" we are giving to you. Let jump into the benefits.

The first benefit is higher earning potential. As you invest in your spouse, the same thing with your degree, you're going to get a higher earning potential. Some of things we earn in marriage in emotional, spiritual, relational, and even sexual dividends

Next, is better opportunities. When you increase your education, you are exposed to new opportunities for careers. As your increase your education on your spouse, it opens new opportunities to connect, play, and even grow oneness with them.

Another benefit you see is security. If I learn new skill sets, I bring security to my job or career path. When you invest in learning about somebody which is investing your life in somebody, they're going to want to stay with you.

Lastly there is satisfaction. When I made the investment into a career I enjoy there is a deep satisfaction. Also with making a investment into my spouse, you see a deep satisfaction relationally, practically, sexually, etc. that will last for a lifetime.

Shocking truth: In a recent survey of betrayed spouses conducted by a recovery center, the concept of trust/how to recapture that sacred commodity was by far the most asked question. In fact, the issue of trust was raised almost twice as much as any other question or concern.

That's huge. If you're not investing in a doctorate in your spouse, you're putting it somewhere else, and that's why trust wanes away. When I'm focusing on my spouse full time, those things are not going to happen. Trust is not going to be an issue.

I've (Daniel) deployed with the military four times. I've not had a specific trust issue with my wife because I'm continually investing in her.

What's the contrast? As God knows us and we desire to know Him, our relationship with Him deepens. He calls us to love Him and to love others. When we don't nurture our spouses, it will grow the distance, which will in the long run have our spouses leave us in one form or another. (emotionally, spiritually, physically).

What's a doctorate degree? A doctorate degree is the highest level of academic degree. Everyone is familiar with the medical doctors, who hold an MD, but you can earn a doctorate in almost any subject, so let's study our spouses. We're going to dive in to do that.

How do we go over and do that particular thing? One recommendation, especially for you non-readers, is read books on communication. Our foundation in any relationship is communication, which we learn from observing via trial/error. We want you to Learn & Live, so doing this trial/error is a no-go. Communication is 55% body language, 38% tone, and 7% verbal. Just understanding this fact alone is one of the first key to absorb on the path to a "thriving" relationship. As we are communicating with each other, we need to be observers rather than thinking our next thought or interrupting. The average person interrupts in 17 seconds or less. As for recommendations, they will be listed below in your action plan

Next thing, we need to go over to get a doctorate in your spouse is shared activities/events. There are three types of ways to connect when sharing activities. We've got face to face, Ladies tend to thrive/want this most often. Guys tend to shy away from this form because it is the most intimate form. This form is shared when going out to eat, meeting for coffee, walking. Most in-depth knowledge of your spouse can be learned at this time. Just like a interview or business meeting, this face to face time activities can also make or break decisions. This should be the most important form of shared activites with your spouse to grow in your "doctrine" degree.

Shoulder to Shoulder is the next form of shared activities, Guys typically thrive in this form of shared activity. From working in the car, play sports, working on a project, to watching sports/tv show is the way to connect. This shared experience build friendships, memories, and bonds people. That is why sports and military personnel have the deepest relationships. When they share the same experiences together it builds a bond that can't be broken. If you want to build tight relationships with your spouse and build intimacy this is one way to earn your degree fast. Lastly is back to back activities. These are typically when a project or mission needs to be complete. An example is tacking house chores. Each of you is doing a different part to accomplish the overall goal. This is the least effective so be sure to reconnect face to face for praise/rewards. If the execution and reward is planned well, you can deeper your knowledge/respect for one another.

When we take the time for activities/events, you will grow your ties together even if you don't see it in the immediate. I (Daniel) in regards to zip lining, is one of those things I wanted to avoid like the plague. I don't like being high; I don't like moving fast, I don't like using a leather glove to break my body at 50 miles per hour while my body is hanging from a cable. I was so scared. Not my idea of a good time. But it was the best time to go over to connect with my wife, and it brought a greater intimacy. As for Michelle she hates reading, so to compromise and to know me better she listens to me read. This connects with me deeply.

Our last suggestion is marriage retreats. Most of "academic learning" of our spouse happens by accident as we share life experiences. On the job training is great but you will only get surface deep and not learn much about the "heart". In marriage retreats, this is the time you could focus your time, intentionally get to know your spouse while recharging your batteries. This takes extensive planning, finances, time, etc. There are several options across the nation which can fit your specific needs. If you need particular sources, you can just e-mail us, and we will find you the best resource for those retreats. Here is a freebie if you are both Christians (because of nature of the focus, Christians couples would enjoy this the most. Anyone can go but we think non-religious couples would feel weird in this environment.) There's a great place called the Billy Graham Evangelistic Association in Ashville North Carolina. If you're military, they give you two free military retreats a year. People like Tommy Nelson, Chip Ingram, Dr. Gary Chapman, etc. are the keynote speakers for the weekend. Additionally, they cover almost everything (excluding travel/childcare) From the 100 acre landscape tucked in the mountains of North Carolina, to the staff, the rooms, food, and the connection is just a few reasons we recommend this place.

My sheep listen to my voice. "I know them, and they follow me. I give them eternal life, and they shall never perish; no one can snatch them out of my mind"

John 10:27-28

The great objections/responses:

1) "I hate reading and studying. I went to school for 12 years; I'm done with school. If I don't have to read and I don't have to review, I'm not going to do that." Well, in this day/age you can access audio books and videos to help you glean/grow. There are so many different ways to learn nowadays that there's no excuse. Go get your diploma. It's you. I'm just going to say it point blank; it was the same thing with me. There was nobody else; it was me.

2) "We're on a fixed income, and it's hard to share time outside of the home with the kids." We can relate and understand that. We're at a place right now, ranging my military duty/freelance work/ publishing this book/etc We know all types of social economic status . As a consumer world, we typically have 10-20% of discretionary income (i.e eating out, shopping, Starbucks, etc).The average American family eats out 2-3 times a day now. It's pretty crazy. We challenge to evaluate you budget/time to make this a priority. If you need more ideas, connect with us.

3)"Retreats are expensive, hard to plan, plus it takes away from the family". Retreats range from 50 bucks to thousands of dollars, depending on the location, length, etc. The average divorce thousands of dollars a year.(court fees, lose hours a week dealing with the new life patterns, tax benefits, etc). If money is not your issue, then think about this way. What legacy do you want to leave your family? If we always just have family time, then this shows your kids that they are most important. When your kids see you put God, spouse, kids, in this priority order you will build better legacies for your kids' marriages, grandkids, so on and so forth. The impact is huge. If you have an average four kids in ten generations, you're going to impact 250,000 people. With six kids it's at 10 million. Just something to chew on for a bit.

Being known is the bricks,
being connected is the cement

-Anshar Martin

ULTRAPRENEURSAYINGS.COM

Action time!!!

1) Go to our Resources page for additional book recommendation and/or contact us for additional contextualized resources for your life season. We what to give you the best, so let us get to know you via FB/call/text.

2) Have a quick chat each week and plan an event to share some learning time with your spouse. Ask these type of questions: What have you been studying? What have you been learning? What have you been learning about me?

3) Look at your calendar to schedule a marriage retreat. Again here are a few places to "google" that we recommended. The Billy Graham Evangelistic Center (www.thecove.org) and also "Weekend to Remember". We want you to choose what's best for you so if these don't work, connect with us and we will help you find a great resource (either us or someone else). We want to thrive in your marriage. That is our heart.

Go get your doctorate degree in your spouse. Get off this chapter and go start studying. All right.

Let's finish the race via the last chapter.

Thrive on!!!

CHAPTER 12

Thrive Not Survive

The question is not how to survive, but how to thrive with passion, compassion, humor, and style.

-MAYA ANGELOU

This chapter is about legacy. We all want that for our lives but little of us know how to achieve it. When we're succeeding, we can thrive towards our legacy. When we're surviving, we're lose our drive to head for legacy. When we are going towards the inheritance that God is calling us for, you will see five benefits that we go over and see.

When you're going towards your legacy, you have a purpose. Purpose goes over and keeps you going. Legacy provides a mission which gives you energy and reason why you're here. Also, it provides direction. You're not just going aimless and shooting in different directions. Most people go shallow and wide pursuing life. A person pursuing legacy goes narrow and deep. Legacy gives you passion. Now you know what you're called to do so passion drives you. Lastly you gain a compassion. A compassion to love people that God's calling you to love on.

Our last fact and statistic and shocking truth:(drum roll). As of 2013, the word legacy is currently in the top 1% of lookups and is the 131st most popular word on the Merriam Webster website.

What's the contrast? What does it look like when we don't have a legacy, and we don't have a purpose? When we just survive in our marriage, we're only on autopilot. When trials come our way, it lets the enemy win with ease. It is a battlefield for our souls, our minds, our hearts and our body. Surviving enables the enemy to get what he wants, gets you away from God, your spouse, your kids, and the legacy that he has for you. A marriage legacy shows the holy power of God in our lives and to others.

What is a legacy? What does it mean? Our definition that we came up with:(this is not the definition from Webster) Legacy is a mission or message left behind in one's memory. It is on the mind of all God's people to thrive in him, which entails a legacy. We need to discover how an individual legacy can become a couple's quest. How do we go over and do that? We have only four, but these are very powerful.

1) Prepare like you're running a marathon. What do I mean by that? A marriage over time will have several trials. For ourselves, we've survived Michelle almost dying, we've had 3/4 of the kids nearly die, we've been borderline homeless four times, 35 moves in 35 years, mental health issues, etc. Most of these are over (Praise God) but trials are a "when" not a "if". on that. Like the marathon you know at certain points you will hit hard spots like "Mile 8 and 18". We can prepare for it

One way to prepare for the legacy race, it to glean off "runners" of the past to have a great race. In regard to marriage, this can be a pastor, godly couple. Marriage consultant or marriage counselor to name a few. Couples that receive pre-marital advice are 30% less likely to get divorced. Additionally, during the marriage race, you might a tune up too. As runners, hydrate and grab power snack during the run, you too need to regularly check in with one of these resources to see how your marriage is doing. Don't wait until you hit a major problem. It is always easier to maintain than to fix.

2) Take care of yourselves. Stewardship is the conducting, supervising or managing something. Especially the careful and responsible management of something entrusted to one's attention. A martial legacy is a gift and we need to steward it well. We are interested in what God gives us to manage well, and our spouses are included. When we took our vows, it was showing us that we're supposed to be stewarding the person in all seasons of life.

There are several realms of stewardship and here are a few: physical health, mental health, emotional well being, spiritual formation, finances, time, energy management, sexual intimacy, the household, parenting, etc. This list can go on and on, and this list is extensive. Men, if you call yourself to Jesus this extensive list is part of legacy we are privileged to lead on. This principle is daunting. Remember there are three people in every marriage, and as we are faithful, He will sustain you in that time.

As we take on this stewardship role, I highly recommend you do an inventory in these areas to evaluate your strong/weak areas. Then, plan to talk about successes together and areas of improvement. This behavior is going to help you thrive by learning to give praise, deliver constructive criticism, fight well, and prayer together.

3) Find your master, mission, and mate. If you've already

found one or if you've discovered one, spur on your spouse to locate the rest. The way I saw my master was in 2002 when God brought me to himself. (If you don't know Jesus, I would love to talk to you and show you how to find him) In 2005, via a quick sermon in Switzerland on "My master, My mission, My mate". I learned that I didn't have a mission(legacy) so I stopped dating to figure that out. God brought my mate to me to marry on December 18th of 2006, which is excellent. My specific mission (Learn & Live) was brought me in 2007. God kept me here to teach the world better relationships. That's what We are doing with Learn & Live. Helping you to "Thrive Not Survive".

Sometimes we do these things not in order; my wife is finding her mission, she clarified a bit more with me today. And how it aligns with mine, so I encourage her to continue, search and find. You don't want to force people into a specific mission. If it doesn't work with your kids, it doesn't work with adults. (spouse) You also need a safe environment in doing that for your spouse. I (Daniel) didn't provide a safe place for a long time. In 2013, it almost destroyed my marriage. We need our master the most, which will be the glue to hold things together. If you and your spouse don't know your master, pray for the other and serve them well until the Lord does his work. We can pray for you in our Learn and Live support group on Facebook. If both of you don't know your master, we recommend the Case for Faith/Case for Christ by Lee Strobel. This publication is an overview to know Jesus in a logical and practical way. Now there is a movie for "The Case for Christ". Either resource is a great tool to learn about faith in Christ.

Our recommendation to find your mission is these three tools. As you're finding your purpose in Christ, you should take a personality assessment, spiritual gifts test, and schedule a consultation. These tools will help you understand your natural and spiritual gifts with a guide helping you along the way. After equipping yourself with Jesus and finding your mission (legacy) you are ready to look for your mate. We recommend a personality assessment, consultation, and reading "The Sacred Search" by Gary Thomas. This book will reorient your thinking, how to find your soul mate in the right way while also understand how to get other with others in a practical way.

4)Our last recommendation: (strong emphasis) is avoid sarcasm at all costs. Sarcasm is a form of offensive language. What does offensive language do? It divides and conquers, stings, aggravates, retaliates, controls, annihilates, shames and manipulates. We think sarcasm is a joke, but it's a lie, and it hurts all of us, and even if we laugh about it or banter back with it, it's damaging.

Persevere: To persist in anything undertaken: maintain a purpose in spite of difficulty, obstacles, or discouragement; continue steadfastly

My wife showed me that I was very sarcastic, and I know I told this story in the other parts of the book, but I think it resonates too. Continuing to be sarcastic in the early years tore my wife apart. Her exact words to describe this torture was "It's like a razor cut to my body". God opened my eyes that night by showing me her in an anatomic position getting cut everywhere across her body and crying 'why'. This gave me the reality of what sarcasm is. Sarcasm translates to vicious which translates to tearing of flesh.

We do it all the time. Lay it down, give it to Jesus to thrive in your life, leave a legacy of healthy marriage. This one thing will have not just your marriage thrive, with time all your relationships will thrive in changing this principle.

Our last objections for the time being. Congratulations to you guys making it to the end

1)" I don't have a godly couple to glean off. We have little friends we can trust in that realm in life." Most older couples in the church are praying to be a mentor for you. Pray for yourself to be bold to ask for it. Also, there are marriage consultants like ourselves, that can work with you short term or long term. Find someone personally or professionally you can trust. We are here to help you find that source of strength for you to thrive

2)" There are so many areas that need to change with me or us, I don't know where to begin?" Usually the problem we run into the most, should be the one we should tackle first. If you don't see it, choose a safe time/place with your spouse to share an area of growth you can explore. Be prepared this might hit you hard. Do not fight, blamshift, or avoid the topic. It will not help but only hinder. To the spouse sharing the area of growth, Don't use "you are" statements because this will lead to defensiveness or arguments. Use "I feel" Statements. (I feel annoyed when you are nagging me on the dishes. This shuts me down and feel less apt to finish them.)

3) "We are all sarcastic, and it doesn't hurt anyone". I thought that too for a long time until God showed me through my wife. This revealed the pain I gave to her and any others my sarcasm hit. It is subtle, however, over time it will build. Some people will explode, break down, cry, get hurt, or push on someone else. We are not meant to take the effects of sin in. Just watch people's reaction to the sarcasm, and you'll see. I(Daniel) have seen too many marriages destroyed from that

and I would have lost mine also if I didn't stop.

One of the authors at the "Ultimate 48 Hour Author" conference told me that her husband did that for 17 years. I thank her for the advice because now I can give it to you, so we can "Learn & Live". The sarcasm doesn't help us succeed, it barely keeps us in surviving mode and eventually kills us.

Our last few actions that you as the reader should take because of reading this chapter.

1) Take the time this month to pray and search for a godly couple, coach or consultant to help you walk through this thing called marriage. It will be fruitful.

2) Evaluate your stewardship via self-reflection. Ask your spouse the top area you can improve.

3) If you don't know your mission, take a personality assessment with us, download a spiritual gifts test and schedule a consultation with us. We'd love to get to know you too and help you get to your goals and dreams and as a couple.

4) Choose a day this week to not be sarcastic for the day. It's going to be hard; especially us guys. See if it makes a difference in how your day goes. Ask for responses from the people you love and even coworkers on your sarcasm? "Google" The verbal enemy at the gate article at www.lifeway.com for a more in-depth talk on this topic.

You've reached the end of our entire book. Congrats!!!

We wanted to pray for you before you depart.

Jesus, thank you for the opportunity to love these people that are reading this book. We hope this resource helped them give their marriage back to you, so it can thrive in the legacy that you're called to be. I thank you for the time that you allowed us to share with them our hearts. We pray that our sacrifice helps their marriages to thrive. If you will it, we can meet to help them more in a practical way.

In the strong name of Jesus Christ

Amen.

Blessing to you and "thrive in Him"

Daniel & Michelle Faust

HOW WE CAME TOGETHER

AND THIS BOOK

Michelle was a home town girl raised in Gig Harbor via her parents. Even though her home wasn't the best home, Jesus grabbed her at the tender age of 4 years. She was able to survive because of her faith and fighting spirit. She left her house at 16 to live with friends and eventually signed up with a church for a internship. Daniel was raised in a sorta moral home but not with Jesus. After his parents got a divorce and his brother died in a 18 month period, he left all moral following and dive into the Wiccan faith. Years later he signed up for the U.S Air Force to travel the world while avoiding the pain of these two traumatic events. After 6 years in he got sent to Washington which he met Michelle. They got married quickly and quickly found out that without Jesus and understanding of your spouse a marriage can spiral quickly to divorce. When a deployment came, Daniel was wrestling with divorce and God brought a awesome chaplain and a book Michelle sent to him called "Positive Personality Profiles" to bring scripture and their relationship alive.

This book is a culmination of healing and revelation over the years. Our heart is to Leave No Marriage, Family, and Veteran behind. Daniel & Michelle have been married for 11 years with four small kids ranging from 7-10 years. They live in Scottsdale, AZ. Come visit us if you are in the area.

623-321-4180

INFO@LEARN-N-LIVE.US

MEET THE AUTHORS

DANIEL & MICHELLE · FAUST ·

FAVORITE COLOR

MICHELLE = BLUE

DANIEL = GREEN

ASK DANIEL ABOUT ONE HANDED CLAPPING OR MICHELLE ON HER VEIN TRICK

HOMETOWN

MICHELLE = GIG HARBOR, WA

DANIEL = CENTRAL FALLS, RI

LEARN & LIVE

Learn & Live

Scottsdale, AZ

623-321-4180

INFO@LEARN-N-LIVE.US

Call /E-mail for our current availability

LIMITED SLOTS

We love to serve you in person or online via being your trainer, keynote speaker, or presenter. Our heart is to "Leave No Marriage Behind" by sharing our lives, testimonials, joys, tears, jokes, and a little one hand clapping with your audience. If you are looking for a breath of fresh air and a good time while learning & growing, we are your dynamic duo. From a couple retreat to an amphitheater of folks, we can adapt to your size of audience.

CALL OR E-MAIL US FOR A PRE-SCREEN INTERVIEW TO SEE IF WE ARE A GREAT MATCH FOR YOUR TEAM, CHURCH, OR ORGANIZATION.

623-321-4180

Info@learn-n-live.us

DANIEL & MICHELLE AS SPEAKERS

Learn & Live

Scottsdale, AZ

623-321-4180

Info@learn-n-live.us

Call /E-mail for our current availability

LIMITED SLOTS

WE ARE AVAILABLE AS KEYNOTE SPEAKERS, PRESENTERS, OR TRAINERS IN THE FOLLOWING AREAS:

MARRIAGE

FAMILY

FAITH

LEADERSHIP

COMMUNICATIONS

WE CONTEXTUALIZE TO ANY SIZE AUDIENCE ONLINE OR IN-PERSON

WANT TO LEARN MORE?

At Learn & Live we know sometimes applying the wisdom our book can take time or sometimes you need a guiding hand from information to transformation. This is where we can step in to assist. We offer consultations on-line, over the phone, or in-person to individuals, couples, families, and groups. No matter if it is 1 session or multiple, we can serve you in this season so you can thrive not just survive. In your unique session, we can dive in deep getting to know you and challenge you to grow and adapt so you can celebrate the cherished relationships.

GIVE US A CALL OR E-MAIL FOR A **FREE** 15 MINUTE CONSULTATION TO **THRIVE!**

623-321-4180

INFO@LEARN-N-LIVE.US

RESOURCES FOR YOU

After you read this book, you are probably saying to yourself " I wish there was a list of the resources, books, websites, etc I could reference in one shot. Well here is snapshot list you can reference from time to time (this is not an exhaustive list. It is just the highlights)

WWW.PERSONALITY-INSIGHTS.COM/?REF=52

This is where you buy all the personality profiles, books, DVD we reference in Ch 2 and Ch 9. You save 10% buying from this direct link and be able to schedule a consultation after purchase.

WWW.DATEBOX.COM

This is a great kit and app that delivers you date ideas to your house on a monthly basis. No contracts and cancel anytime. They have two plans depending on your budget

WWW.SHIPT.COM

This takes the burden of grocery shopping and still gives a quality worker that delivers the exact grocery you are looking for. This will recharge your spouse by saving them 1-2 hrs a week from hitting the grocery stores

BOOK REFERENCES

Positive Personality Profiles (Dr. Robert Rohm)
Who do you think you are anyway? (Dr. Robert Rohm)
The Good Fight (Dr. Les & Leslie Parrott)
The Tyranny of the Urgent (Charles Hummel)
Love & Respect (Dr Emerson Eggerichs)
Real Marriage: The Truth about Sex, Friendship, and Love Together (Mark & Grace Driscoll)
Boundaries in Marriage (Dr.Henry Cloud & Dr. John Townsend)
Body & Soul Understanding your Sexual Personality (Duane Storey & Sanford Kulkin)

*** The dots represent the potential to purchase at our webstore listed at the top of the page***

www.ingramcontent.com/pod-product-compliance
Lightning Source LLC
Chambersburg PA
CBHW031340060726
47590CB00007B/2554